Learning to Listen, Listening to Learn

Building essential skills in young children

Mary Renck Jalongo

National Association for the Education of Young Children
Washington, DC

National Association for the Education of Young Children
1313 L Street NW, Suite 500
Washington, DC 20005-4101
202-232-8777 or 800-424-2460
www.naeyc.org

Learning to Listen, Listening to Learn

Through its publications program, the National Association for the Education of Young Children (NAEYC) provides a forum for discussion of major issues and ideas in the early childhood field, with the hope of provoking thought and promoting professional growth. The views expressed or implied in this book are not necessarily those of the Association or its members.

Carol Copple, *director, Publications & Initiatives in Educational Practice*; Bry Pollack, *managing editor, Books*; Malini Dominey, *design and production*; Cassandra Berman, *editorial associate*; Melissa Edwards, *editorial assistant*; Natalie Klein Cavanagh, *photo editor*

Library of Congress Control Number: 2007938081
ISBN: 978-1-928896-46-3
NAEYC Item #2008

About the Author

Mary Renck Jalongo is a teacher, writer, and editor. Her most recent book for NAEYC was a second edition of *Young Children and Picture Books* (2004).

As a classroom teacher, she taught preschool, first grade, and second grade; worked with children from families of migrant farm workers; and taught in the laboratory preschool at the University of Toledo. Currently she is a professor at Indiana University of Pennsylvania, where she is the coordinator of the doctoral program in Curriculum and Instruction. She has been the recipient of the university's Outstanding Professor Award, as well as numerous other teaching awards and three national awards for excellence in writing. For the past 13 years, she has been the editor-in-chief of the international publication *Early Childhood Education Journal*.

Mary Renck Jalongo has coauthored and edited more than 20 books, many of them textbooks, including *Early Childhood Language Arts* (4th ed., Allyn & Bacon), *Creative Thinking and Arts-Based Learning* (4th ed., Merrill/Prentice Hall), *Exploring Your Role: An Introduction to Early Childhood Education* (3d ed., Merrill/Prentice Hall), and *Major Trends and Issues in Early Childhood Education: Challenges, Controversies, and Insights* (2d ed., Teachers College Press). In addition, she is a contributor to the *World Book Encyclopedia* and the author of two Association for Childhood Education International (ACEI) Position Papers. Recent publications include *Planning for Learning: Collaborative Approaches to Lesson Design and Review* (Teachers College Press, 2006) and *The World's Children and Their Companion Animals: Developmental and Educational Significance of the Child/Pet Bond* (ACEI, 2004).

Contents

Boxes

The Listening Paradox

What I needed as a child in school was a teacher who wanted to hear my voice, my ideas, the words that were always present but never spoken; a teacher who would have given me the support and safety and a space in which to project that voice ... a teacher who would have valued my voice just because it was mine, not because it provided the right answer.
—Karen Gallas

In preparation for writing this book, I revisited my thick file folder of materials collected across many years of thinking, teaching, and writing about listening. Inside was a greeting card signed by all of the teachers enrolled in a long-ago summer workshop. The message, written in calligraphy, read: "What people really need is a good listening to." Attached to the front was a sticky note with two words I had written in my best former-first-grade-teacher printing: "Bryan's story."

Bryan had been a red-headed, freckle-faced boy in my class who was shy, was small for his age, and struggled with reading. He lived with his mother, a substitute teacher in our small, rural elementary school and a single parent. On her way to an interview for a permanent teaching position, Bryan's mother was killed in an auto accident. The night before Bryan was scheduled to return to my classroom, I tossed and turned, worrying about what to do or say in the face of such a tragic loss. An arrangement emerged gradually and almost naturally.

As a novice teacher, I needed extra preparation time and would arrive early and stay late. Bryan began to follow my schedule. During those quiet times before and after school, he would help out around the classroom and sometimes share his concerns in solemn, tentative sentences. From listening to Bryan, I overcame one of my biggest fears, that of saying the wrong thing. I learned that simply giving undivided attention or a sympathetic look as he talked could be just as comforting as my saying the "right" thing. I learned when it was important to speak and when it was better to listen. Bryan stands out in my mind, not only as a child who desperately needed "listening to" but also as one of my great teachers.

Why this book is necessary

Americans tend to be viewed by other cultures as better talkers than listeners, and members of the teaching profession perhaps even more so. As Gilbert (2005) points out, "most people have not been taught the skill of listening. Hence, it is not surprising that most do not do it well. As a result, most do not listen effectively, including the educators who demand their students do it" (2). Studies over the years estimate that some 60–90 percent of the talk in classrooms is produced by one person—the teacher (Jalongo 2006).

Yet if we think back to the best teachers we encountered as children or about our most admired colleagues today, they probably share the attribute of being thoughtful listeners. People who will take the time and trouble to listen not merely with their ears but also with their minds and hearts are a rarity and a treasure. As with the development of so many other types of knowledge, skills, and dispositions, it is early childhood that lays the foundation for effective listening throughout life.

Learning to Listen, Listening to Learn is an effort to raise awareness, provide helpful information, and empower adults who care for and about young children to embrace their role in promoting effective listening, not only in young children but also in themselves. To understand why such a book is necessary, we need only consider these statistics:

- According to the U.S. Census Bureau (2007), Americans spend nearly half of their lives receiving and interpreting messages. In a year, the average person spends the equivalent of 146 days watching TV, going online, listening to the radio or music, or reading. More often than not, listeners multitask.

- On average, people spend 70 percent of their waking hours communicating, three-fourths of them allocated to listening and speaking (Hyslop & Tone 1988; Paul 1996). Despite the predominance of listening, most people get little or no training in listening and nonverbal communication (Timm & Schroeder 2000).

- Of all the language skills that young children develop, listening is the one that develops the earliest and is practiced most frequently (Palmer 2004; Roskos, Christie, & Richgels 2003). In some domains, such as music and literature, listening is the major activity of young children.

- Although listening is the language skill that children (without hearing impairments) use the most in the outside world, it is the one that is taught the least in the classroom (Smith 2003). As a result, listening has been referred to as the neglected or forgotten language art (Tompkins 2005).

- As much as 80 percent of the information learners obtain is the result of listening (Bredekamp 2000), yet listening has been the "orphan of education" for more than 50 years (Imhof 2004).

- Acquiring oral language (i.e., listening and speaking abilities) is so fundamental to functioning in society that it is an important component of "health-related quality of life," or HRQL (Eisenberg, Fink, & Niparko 2006). Listening also is central to the "child's early development of other skills, including survival, social, and intellectual skills" (Wolvin & Coakley 2000, 143).

- Studies conducted on children's listening, both in school and out, estimate that between 50 and 90 percent of children's communication time is devoted to listening (Gilbert 2005; Hunsaker 1990; Norton 2003; Wolvin & Coakley 2000).

- Across the K–12 years, a student might get 12 years of formal training in writing, 6–8 years in reading, 1–2 years in speaking, but just a half year or less in listening (Hyslop & Tone 1988).

Throughout a child's basic education, only about 8 percent of instructional time is devoted to teaching listening skills (Cramond 1998).

- When teachers are asked about the obstacles they face in supporting children's learning today, getting students to listen and focus attention usually ranks high on the list (Jalongo 1995; McInnes et al. 2003), yet few teachers have had any specific preparation for the task (C.B. Smith 2003; Tompkins 2005).

- Listening comprehension is considered one of the skills most predictive of overall, long-term school success (Brigman, Lane, & Switzer 2001). Listening is particularly important in learning to read and write (Bennett-Armistead, Duke, & Moses 2005; Braunger & Lewis 2005; Lonigan 2005). Numerous studies have found that problems with listening comprehension predict difficulties with reading later on, for both typically developing children and children with special needs (Heath & Hogben 2004).

- At the university level, listening is given an average of 7 percent of text space and about the same amount of instructional time, yet 64 percent of a college student's time is devoted to learning through listening (Janusik 2002).

- Employers identify effective listening as one of the top three skills sought in job applicants and a key determinant of promotion. Most businesses and organizations, other than schools, offer training courses that focus specifically on listening skills (Janusik 2002).

So the paradox is this: Although listening is the first language skill to develop and is used the most, and although children's problems with listening are a perennial concern of teachers, relatively little has been done to ensure that listening is understood by parents and families to be a *taught* skill, is included in teachers' academic preparation, or is effectively learned by children (Swain, Harrington, & Friehe 2004).

To address these shortcomings requires clear, research-based recommendations that can guide professional practice. Otherwise, effective listening will continue to be expected to occur automatically, virtually ignored in teacher preparation, and neglected in the early childhood curriculum. In *Teaching of Early Reading: Final Report*, for example, researchers in the United Kingdom offered this as their key recommendation:

> Best practice for beginning readers provides them with a rich curriculum that fosters all four interdependent strands of language: speaking, listening, reading, and writing. The indications are that far more attention needs to be given to promoting speaking and listening skills to make sure that children build a good stock of words, learn to listen attentively, and speak clearly and confidently. Speaking, listening, reading, and writing are central to children's intellectual, social, and emotional development. (Rose 2006, 28)

What may be even more surprising to educators is that some experts believe that in many ways, listening is more difficult to learn than reading is:

> Children learn oral language without formal instruction but are bombarded with assistance in learning to read. Ironically, oral language is actually the greater intellectual feat of the two.... In acquiring oral language, children must first discover the existence and purpose of language, then master its sounds and structure, and finally learn the multitude of oral symbols which constitute vocabulary. In learning to read, children can build on their previous knowledge of their language as they figure out the written symbol system used to represent it. (Fields, Groth, & Spangler 2007, 29)

If you doubt that listening effectively is harder than reading, consider these points:

- Listeners usually have to contend with both verbal *and* nonverbal messages; readers have only a particular text (and possibly pictures) (Imhof 2004). In listening, 90 percent or more of the total impact of a message comes from nonverbal features (i.e., tone of voice and gesture), while only about 7 percent comes from words (Timm & Schroeder 2000).

- Listeners have to adjust to the speaker's pace. Readers control their own pace; they can read difficult material more slowly or even stop and come back to it later.

- Previewing ("look aheads") as well as repair ("look backs") are easier to accomplish when reading than when listening (Imhof 2004).

- "Listening is a dynamic system, so if one part of the system is changed, then the whole system changes" (Janusik 2002, 8); by comparison, a printed text is permanent and controllable.

- Because the ear does not differentiate between the message and noise until *after* the sounds have been processed, a listener is unable to hear only what is important. A reader knows right from the start that all of the text is part of the intended message.

For all of these reasons and more, learning to listen is a formidable challenge—but meeting that challenge is vital if children are to become successful learners.

Children are well aware of the listening/learning connection. When director Connie Kerr Vogt asked the preschoolers in her Reggio Emilia–based program, "How can listening help you?" some of their answers were:

> "You can learn by listening to people talking about things you don't know about, or listen to someone read books, or listen to music and learn the words to the song, or listen to birds and learn about them! Anytime you listen, you can learn."

> "If you're listening, you'll learn everything you hear! If you hear music, and you're really listening to it, you'll dance!"

> "People can tell you things and you can figure things out. Like if your mom or dad or teacher help you sound letters and words out, you have to listen carefully so you can hear it. That's how you learn to say the words you read."

> "You can learn about Mexico and puppies and caterpillars and butterflies and chrysalises and books if you listen. And lots of other things, too!"

> "You can learn by listening. Nature sounds are beautiful; it's nice to listen to birds and rain and even wind. If you listen carefully, you can hear leaves falling!"

As these insights from young children suggest, teaching children to "listen better" is an important obligation of early childhood educators, one that extends across all subject areas. *Learning to Listen, Listening to Learn* was written to support teachers in developing the knowledge, skills, and attitudes they need in order to support the development of children's listening skills.

About this book

To improve young children's listening demands three things of us: an understanding of the listening process; the implementing of research-based teaching strategies; and an appreciation for the changes needed in ourselves, in our classrooms, and in children's homes and communities. The chapters that follow take up each of these.

Although children are expected to listen even more than they are expected to speak, read, or write, *learning* to listen is given scant attention in the early childhood curriculum, and even less in teacher preparation. With this in mind, Chapter 1 reflects on the particular importance of listening for young children, who are relative newcomers to the communication process. Chapter 2 details the many ways in which educators can prepare the classroom environment to create contexts that promote effective listening. Chapter 3 examines challenges to effective listening and suggests pedagogical approaches that meet the needs of diverse groups of learners. Chapter 4 focuses on practical teaching strategies, including integration across the curriculum and assessment. Chapter 5 suggests ways that teachers can work with families to promote effective listening. Chapter 6 urges teachers to take a critical look at their own listening and how it affects daily interactions with young children, parents and families, and colleagues.

Chapter 1

Understanding Listening

Connecting with others is at the heart of communication—defined best as one person understanding what another wants understood. The key to this understanding is listening.

—Michael B. Gilbert

In the folktale, Little Red Riding Hood meets the wolf and remarks, "What big ears you have!" to which the wolf-in-grandma's-clothing replies, "The better to hear you with, my dear." Oversized ears may help us to hear better, but they do not ensure better listening. In fact, sounds can be perceived with complete auditory accuracy, but unless they are connected with *understanding*, listening does not occur. So effective listening begins with hearing, but it certainly does not end there.

At its most basic, *communication* (in which listening plays a major role) requires a sender, a receiver, a message, and a channel or medium. Imagine that two children are conducting a sound experiment with a couple of tin cans connected by a string. The child who is speaking is the *sender*, the child who is straining to hear is the *receiver*, the *message* probably is some version of "Can you hear me now?" and the *medium* is the makeshift telephone line. Of course, the reality of communicating is more complex than that. One feature that makes communication more involved is the need for understanding—not only from the sender, who encodes the message, but also from the receiver, who decodes it. Another feature is that because most communication isn't only one-way, the sender and the receiver must switch roles in turns. Effective communication relies on a feedback loop ("I heard what you said; is this what you meant?") to sustain that understanding throughout the exchange.

Communication—particularly the direct, candid communication of young children—has two purposes: to make sense and to build relationships (Nelson 2007). When young children hear a message, they attempt to make sense of it—as this group of kindergartners did:

> Lori, who had visited a farm over the weekend, said excitedly, "The ewes are lambing!" The other children heard the word *ewes* as "yous," but they couldn't figure out why *you* was plural or what Lori thought they were doing that was called "lambing." It was not until after their teacher explained that a mother sheep is a ewe and that birthing baby sheep is called "lambing" that the other children understood.

Yet the children had tried, using the language they did know, to make sense out of a perplexing message. They had listened to Lori and they had heard what she said (or at least what they *thought* she said), but their prior knowledge of sheep was insufficient for them to understand what she *meant*.

Young children also communicate as a way to initiate and sustain relationships. For example, it is a widely held misconception that children's first words typically are nouns used to label things, such as people, pets, or objects. Actually, many of the one-word utterances of infants and toddlers are used for social interaction (Nelson 2007), such as saying "Hi" to get daddy's attention, "Up" to ask to be picked up, or "Peek" to initiate a game of peek-a-boo with grandpa.

Even when young children do use nouns, the words often are a shorthand way of, again, building relationships and making sense of experience. The toddler who thrusts a picture book into her mother's hands and says "Mama" with a tone of command in her voice is trying to initiate a reading session; when she hears the garage door open and asks "Daddy?" she's trying to interpret the sound she just heard. Even when children's vocabulary is limited to a handful of words, they will use those words to connect and comprehend.

A definition of listening

Listening can be difficult to define because we use the word in everyday conversation to mean different things. Listening consultant Carole Grau notes, for example: If a teacher says to a child, "You're not listening," it often means "You're not thinking along with me"; if a parent says it to a child, it usually means "You're not doing as I say." In an advocacy context, "You're not listening" often means "You're not agreeing with me"; and in a marital one, "You don't listen to me" generally means "You're not recognizing my emotions."

These 4-year-olds who were asked what it means to "listen" focused most of their answers on hearing different sounds:

> "It means to hear what people are saying or babies crying and saying 'Dada' or sometimes you can listen to music."

> "You listen with your ears, you are hearing sounds. Like a bulldozer, or if someone is dumping mulch in your driveway, you can hear the dump truck. It's a rumbling noise that you hear. You can listen to your friends talk to you. Or your mom and dad talk to you."

> "It means to hear something, like people talking or when animals make sounds, or music and dogs barking."

Interestingly, a 5-year-old who had a little bit more experience with listening added another element:

> "Listening means to pay attention, then use your imagination."

As this last child realized, effective listening goes beyond merely receiving sounds. Throughout history, people have appreciated that listening is more than just hearing. The ancient Greeks formed the word for *listen* by placing *hyper* in front of their word for *hear* (*akouein*); so in Greek, *listening* is literally translated as "hearing in great amount" or "intense hearing." Interestingly, the Chinese character for *listen* includes the notions not merely of hearing but also of nonverbal behavior and of connecting with the speaker in cognitive as well as affective ways. Listening is also connected with ideas. For example, the Sino-Japanese character for the word *idea* is the combination of two other characters: "sound" and "heart."

All these linguistic and cultural perspectives on what it means to listen and understand ideas are consistent with contemporary research, which sees listening as something active and complex:

Listening should be viewed as a verb and not a noun. As a verb, it is a process; it is what the listener does. (Janusik 2002, 8)

Listening is the necessary, interactive process that enables the brain to construct meaning from the sounds that are heard. (McSporran 1997, 15)

All that being said, the definition of *listening* used for the purposes of this book is a simple one: **Listening is the process of taking in information through the sense of hearing and making meaning from what was heard.**

In everyday life, the kind of listening we do can run the gamut—from selectively tuning out to hanging on every word and all points in between. Toddler Laura made a deliberate effort to tune out

Hearing vs. Listening: What Are the Distinctions?

Hearing ...	Listening ...
Is a sensory function that develops on its own	Is a cognitive ability that is learned and practiced
Is the act of receiving sounds, and begins even before birth	Is a thought process, and does not begin until children try to interpret the sounds they hear
Depends on physiology in the ear to transmit impulses to the brain	Relies on experience, skill, and practice
Processes sensory input	Comprehends sensory input
Is involuntary and not necessarily focused; we hear many different sounds simultaneously that compete for attention	Is very focused and intentional; we have to become aware, filter out distractions, and focus attention
Does not necessarily have a specific purpose	Occurs when there is a clear purpose in mind
Can often be improved through technology (augmentative and assistive devices)	Can be improved through practice and training
Often declines in older adults and needs to be augmented	Often benefits from the patience and wisdom of advancing age

Learning to Listen, Listening to Learn

when her grandmother tried to talk with her about "being a big girl and using the potty." Laura's reply was to wave and say, "Goodbye, Grandma," as she closed the bathroom door. It is also possible to only pretend to be listening ("Mmmm hmmm") or to listen selectively ("Did somebody say *ice cream*?").

The kind of listening that teachers most need to help young children learn to do, however, is *effective listening*. When listening effectively, we are:

- *receiving*—taking in the verbal or nonverbal message

- *attending to*—engaging effort and desire to keep our attention focused completely on the message

- *assigning meaning*—interpreting or understanding the message through cultural contexts and personal intellectual and emotional processes (Wolvin & Coakley 1996)

When we are being effective listeners, we also are using specific tools and strategies; we filter out distractions, process information thoughtfully, make pertinent comments, and ask relevant questions (Brent & Anderson 1993).

Ways of listening

Think of a memorable message that you listened to with great intensity. Here are a few examples offered by teachers:

> "My granddaughter, who is 14 months old, is just starting to talk. I just love hearing her sweet little voice and was thrilled when she called me Grammy."

> "When my husband said, 'Guess what? I got five out of six numbers on the lottery ticket. I have to look it up to see how much it's worth.' It was over $1,000!"

> "I took my mother for her 6-month check-up after her surgery and listened to the doctor give her prognosis. I was holding my breath, waiting to hear the words 'no sign of cancer' and 'it looks like we got it all.' And I am so thankful that he did say them."

As these examples illustrate, not only do we listen and learn, we also listen and *feel*. Listening can bring us joy (e.g., from words of love or beautiful music), but also hurt and sorrow (e.g., from a cruel remark or news of a loved one's death). Although we hear thousands of words spoken every day that quickly fade from memory, certain pieces of language are indelibly printed on our minds. Usually, those unforgettable messages remain because they triggered an emotional *response*.

The point is, when adults speak about children's listening, we generally mean more than just hearing, and more even than comprehending. We also mean *responding* appropriately. The International Listening Association agrees, offering the following as its official definition:

> Listening is the process of receiving, constructing meaning from, and responding to spoken and/or nonverbal messages. (1995, 4)

By "responding" we mean that listeners get involved with the message intellectually or emotionally or both. Four ways of listening are:

Hearing is a physiological response that includes *auditory acuity* (the ability to hear sounds) and *auditory perception* (the mental abilities to discriminate among individual sounds, to blend sounds together, and to hold sequences of sounds in memory). The brain's auditory center needs a clear and complete signal for children to understand what they hear.

Interpreting is a response of perception that includes *focusing, becoming aware,* and *selecting cues* from the environment. For example,

> A group of preschoolers was listening to a story in the university child care center when the reader asked, "What does it mean to *tease*? Has anyone ever teased you?" A solemn 4-year-old offered, "It's when someone says, 'Here's a very nice toy for you,' but then they take it away and say, 'Nyah, nyah, nyah. You can't have it.'"

Interpreting consists of getting meaning from what is heard, relating it to something already known, then organizing, imagining, and thinking about what was heard. Clearly, this preschooler understood the reader's questions, connected them with her personal experience, and used that experience to arrive at a very accurate definition. The other children listened to her example, understood it, and supplied examples of their own:

> One boy remarked, "Yeah, like when a big kid steals your hat and keeps throwing it at the wall so it sticks to the bricks." Another child said, "My sister's boyfriend teased me. He said they were going to see Big Bird and I couldn't go, but it was the [grocery] store Giant Eagle, not like *Sesame Street*."

Evaluating combines listening with specialized expertise. For example, an audience with limited musical experience might hear and judge a singer's performance based on generic factors such as the singer's enthusiasm or how close the rendition is to a version the audience knows. In contrast, expert judges might hear and evaluate the technical difficulty of the song, the singer's vocal skills against a standard, and the originality of the interpretation. Music educators Johnson and Koga are talking about responding at this level when they say, "We hear these contrasts [in performance] on the concert stage … and even when we listen to young children as early as age 6" (2006/2007, 22). The point here is that Johnson and Koga's specialized expertise allows them to hear a "memorable, moving" performance, versus a merely "technically impressive" one, even when the performer is still very young. Evaluative listening relies on a set of criteria that has been developed and internalized during the process of acquiring the expertise.

Taking action occurs when listening is used to guide the listener's behavior. Judit Szente describes a boy who had been having violent temper tantrums since the start of school:

> As he walked by, the teacher overheard the child ask himself aloud, "What's wrong with me?" When she spoke privately with the boy, he confided, "I think that I am bad." The teacher asked him why, and he said it was because he didn't listen to the teacher, did things he should not do, and got into trouble. Together, teacher and child arrived at a solution that included two positive substitute thoughts: "I can listen" and "I can pay attention to the teacher." (Szente 2007, 451)

In this example, listening became a way to achieve a meeting of the minds and to coach the child in learning the skills of self-regulation. Listening was the basis for a more appropriate behavioral response.

Should we be concerned about children's listening?

At a recent conference, sponsored by a local NAEYC chapter, a session on listening drew 83 early childhood educators. To start things off, the participants were asked to write a statement of their concerns on an index card. A quick tally revealed that more than 90 percent were convinced that today's young children have unprecedented problems with listening:

> "Children today just don't want to listen."

> "I find myself constantly reminding children to pay attention."

> "I am concerned that listening skills are at an all-time low."

> "The media influence is there. Kids are so accustomed to channel surfing on TV or surfing the Net that they can't pay attention for more than a few seconds."

Let's look at what data and experience have to say about some assumptions, beliefs, and misconceptions about children's "problems" with listening.

"I think children just don't listen like they used to."

Asked, "Are you a good listener? How can you tell?" a 4-year-old girl said, "I'm very good at listening. I can feel inside my body that I know what people are saying to me. It's hard to describe. I just know it inside. I know what they are saying, and I understand it." As this child's thoughtful response illustrates, with training and practice, children realize that listening is more than keeping still and remaining quiet; they know that comprehension is the key.

Usually, when teachers remark that listening skills are declining, what they actually mean is that they believe they were better listeners when they were young than children are today, and that as adults they are even better now. Although it is possible for listening skills to improve with time and experience, this is not necessarily the case. A classic work in the field of listening found that 90 percent of first-graders could repeat what had been said during a lecture, while only 28 percent of senior high students could do so (Nichols & Stevens 1957a; 1957b). Teachers also complain that "many adolescents enter high school unprepared to act like students—to sit still and listen, take notes, study on their own, engage in class work, and finish homework" (Darling-Hammond & Ifill-Lynch 2006, 8).

But adults fare no better. Only about 10 percent of Americans listen properly (Timm & Schroeder 2000), and adults (without hearing impairments) listen at about 25–50 percent efficiency (Hunsaker 1990). Just think about how you and your colleagues respond during a required inservice training day. Usually, the leader has to request that cell phones be turned off and laptops, text messaging, email, newspapers, and other reading materials be put away. Even so, a few will succumb to these distractions.

Although it may be hard to admit, when it comes to listening, we sometimes ask children to do as we say, not as we do. In addition, we may be expecting too much: "Teachers who prefer imparting information through lecture require students to listen carefully and well. Many of these teachers see the world through their thoughts and beliefs. Their reliance on listening suggests that students already know how to listen. In reality, few do know how to listen" (Gilbert 2005, 2). The key is to teach children these listening skills—rather than taking them as a "given"—and to practice the skills *ourselves* in all of our interactions.

Tough Questions to Ask Ourselves about "Children's" Listening Problems

Rather than assuming that the fault for children's listening problems rests with them, we need to ask ourselves some tough questions:

- What efforts do I make to be clear and concise with my instructions and to make certain that children understand me?
- Do I remember to state the purpose for listening, so children can appreciate why it is important to pay attention?
- Is the push to cover the curriculum causing me to race through material and talk too much, causing some children to listen marginally or to tune out?
- Do I communicate that listening is valued, not only through my words but also through my actions?
- Can children manage to get by in my classroom without listening carefully because abbreviated answers to low-level questions are the norm?
- Do I set developmentally appropriate expectations for the amount of time that children are expected to listen?
- Am I truly a "listening enthusiast"? For example, do I readily remember the charming, amusing, and poignant things that children say?

"Children's attention spans are shorter, right?"

A 3-year-old boy considered himself to be a good listener, "Because I always stay at my center until the teacher says I can change. When I hear her say it's time to change centers, then I do it—because I listened." If children sense the value in careful listening—in this case, to participate in interesting activities and to be regarded as a responsible student—then they are far more likely to concentrate. Interestingly, the same adults who complain that children cannot attend to a task for more than a few minutes often remark also that children beg to hear the same story over and over again or become totally absorbed in their play. So if it's not that children *can't* focus, what might the problem be?

When teachers rely on talk to the exclusion of other, more interactive approaches, they inadvertently become the cause of children's inattention. Few young children prefer or learn best through the auditory mode alone, and their frustration may cause them to seek negative ways to get their learning needs met (Gilbert 2005). Young children often prefer visual and kinesthetic approaches, and through careful planning, a teacher can complement listening activities with images and physical activities. Doing this can have a remarkable, positive effect on children's listening behaviors and attention spans.

"It's that children don't listen when I tell them to."

A 5-year-old girl remarked, "I am a good listener. When teachers call on me, I always give an answer or I know what they mean." As this child correctly concluded, listening effectively involves more than responding to a teacher's request to "Listen up." With so many sounds and messages competing for attention, listening does depend to a considerable extent on the ability of the listener to ignore much of what is heard. It has been rightly said that teaching is more than telling, and telling children to listen does not teach them how to listen or what to listen for. Children become better listeners when, for example, they are called on to *use* the message they have heard in some meaningful way.

Simply reminding them to listen is ineffective because it does not provide a focus or a goal. Although "selective hearing" sometimes is used in a derogatory way (meaning that a person hears only what he or she *wants* to hear), listening well actually does require selectivity. To identify for children exactly what they are to listen *for* is far more effective than vague, general reminders are. For example,

> A librarian was to speak to Mrs. Rivera's second-graders. To prepare them, she said, "Our guest today is Ms. Melissa. She is the librarian at the public library near our school. Today she is going to talk about how you can participate in Summer Reading Club. I want everyone to listen carefully to find out how you get a library card and how you can earn free books and prizes for reading good books this summer."

Note that her message made children aware of the payoff for listening. Contrast this with,

> "Ms. Melissa is the librarian. Please give her your full attention."

That sort of announcement offers no reason to listen, nor does it help children to focus on the key elements of the message. Likewise, instructions such as these put all of the emphasis on controlling the body rather than focusing the mind:

> "Sit up straight, feet on the floor, hands folded, and eyes up here. The librarian is going to talk to you."

When we ask for children's attention, the first question we must answer for them should be "Attention to what, exactly?" and the second should be "What are the benefits of making the effort to focus and concentrate?"

"Children won't look at me when I'm speaking."

A 4-year-old girl considered herself to be a good listener, "Because I look at people when they talk to me and I am quiet." Although these behaviors are commendable, looking at a speaker does not necessarily lead to listening comprehension. What teacher hasn't had the experience of assuming a child who appeared distracted was not listening, only to find that the child had heard and understood every word.

It is true that many cultures expect listeners to keep their eyes on the speaker as a way of maintaining attention or being courteous. But as teachers we need to be aware that, although the dominant culture may prize direct eye contact, other cultures might regard this as a sign of disrespect. Insisting that children stare at the speaker does not guarantee that listening will occur; it also may run counter to how children are expected to behave at home and in their communities.

Where we look as listeners also depends on the situation. A 5-year-old boy explained, "When people talk to me, I try to remember to look in their eyes. Except if someone is reading a chapter book to me, I look away or close my eyes so I can picture what I'm listening to in my mind." As this child realized, effective listeners can deliberately look away or close their eyes without compromising listening comprehension. Doing this can help them focus on what they are hearing by blocking out visual distractions, such as when we reflect on a surprising idea, close our eyes to enjoy music, or weigh the evidence of someone's argument.

"Children can't have been listening to me, because they get it wrong."

Perhaps you have seen the Internet video of a baby who names all the U.S. presidents. While it is remarkable he can produce them on cue, he's clearly too young to have the slightest idea what he is saying. As this child's behavior illustrates, listening then repeating back—even remembering later—a string of words does not necessarily mean that the listener understands the underlying concepts. Recalling from memory is a very basic listening skill. A better check on children's listening comprehension than having them parrot back is asking them to put what you said into their own words.

A different error comes from children's efforts to make sense out of what they think they hear, such as the child who referred to coleslaw as "cold slop" or who called a pasture a "grassture." These children understand the underlying concepts perfectly—the invented words are clear evidence of that. Limited experience with the language is their problem. The check, however, is the same as before—for the teacher to invite children to talk, and then to listen closely to what they say.

Conclusion

A colleague told me that her 3-year-old son was on his way to preschool when he remarked thoughtfully, "Mom, I think that dogs must be sad ... because they can't go to school." Not long afterward, she, her son, and I were out together and we happened upon a dog training class at the park. The preschooler was captivated by all the activity as well as the different colors, sizes, and shapes of dogs represented. Several dogs barked, a few growled, and many owners urged their animals to behave. This seemed like the perfect opportunity to address the child's comment, so I said, "Guess what? This is school for dogs. What do you think dogs need to learn at school?" The child replied, "How to be nice!"

The boy had not only heard sounds, he had made meaning from them and evaluated the situation—the dogs were not being nice to each other. He also used the listening experience to take action, and a detailed discussion of school for dogs ensued on the way home. As this situation illustrates, there is much that adults can do in terms of attitudes and strategies to foster children's listening skills.

Setting a Context for Listening

What we need is not better teacher talk, but less teacher talk if we are to increase pupil learning.

—Thom Murray and John Swartz

Two 4-year-olds were taking a break from playing school and began to discuss the behavior of their two preschool teachers. "Ms. Amy and Ms. Maura, they, you know, talk a lot. But they should talk to *us*." … "Yeah, we have to be quiet but they talk—that's not fair! 'Cause we're kids and they're teachers they gotta talk to us." Interestingly, these very young children arrived at the same conclusion as many researchers: Teachers need to create the conditions that improve classroom listening in order for children to listen and learn.

What do children gain by listening?

Maria Montessori considered the ability to focus to be one of the great markers of a quality education. Simply reminding children to listen is not enough; with all of the distractions and competition for children's attention, we need to help them focus and guide them in determining what it is they should listen *for* (Funk & Funk 1989). Without focus, learning proceeds in a slow and uncertain fashion.

As a first step in helping young children to become better listeners, consider three main reasons for listening: (1) to think and learn, (2) to act appropriately, and (3) to value and appreciate. Each of these reasons is explained below (Garman & Garman 1992).

1. Listening to obtain information, learn, and develop thinking skills

Children do, in fact, learn by listening, because language is fundamental to perception, memory, thinking, and behavior (Tomasello 2003). By adulthood, most of us can listen at the rate of about 125–250 words per minute and think at 1,000–3,000 words per minute (International Listening Association 2005). People can listen and think about four times faster than others can talk, which gives efficient listeners plenty of time to interpret a message as they hear it (Bell 2000).

Professor Audrey Rule and her colleagues demonstrated the link between listening and thinking in dialogues they recorded in their classroom as children (ages 3–5) guessed what "mystery object" a cardboard box concealed. (See the box on pages 26–27.) As the dialogues illustrate, the success of the children's questioning strategies is dependent upon their listening to one another and to the teacher. Activities such as this mystery box game can help children listen to think and learn—to develop their listening skills and become clearer, better thinkers in the process (Rule 2007).

2. Listening to make decisions, recognize danger, and react or act upon

Jason, a student teacher working toward initial teacher certification, was presenting a lesson on safety to a classroom of 22 kindergartners. Formerly a state police officer, Jason had experience making presentations on safety to auditoriums full of elementary school children. Now that he had the opportunity to work with a group he knew well, Jason was eager to try something more interactive and memorable than a large group presentation would have been.

He began by lining up chairs and asking the children to pretend that the chairs were seats on the big yellow bus. Six children at a time got to be passengers, while the remaining students, seated in a semi-circle on the floor, decided whether the behaviors demonstrated by the passengers were safe or not. As the first group of passengers assembled, he took them aside and whispered instructions: "Now, I want you to yell and wave out the bus windows." He also asked one child to very carefully stand on the chair. As the scene unfolded, Jason asked, "How are they doing?" and a child in the audience replied, "Not very good!" Jason prompted, "Okay, what's wrong here?" Children responded with comments such as, "You have to stay in your seat" … "No hands or things out the window" … "They're *way* too noisy." As each comment was offered, he asked that child why the behaviors were problematic.

It was clear that the children knew why—"You shouldn't stand up because you might fall if the bus driver has to stop" … "You shouldn't hang anything out the window because you might drop it, or if it's your hand it could hit something outside like a tree" … "You shouldn't be screaming because the bus driver needs to hear trains, horns, ambulances, and fire engines." Afterward Jason reflected in his teaching log,

> "I was really impressed with how well the children did. They didn't just memorize and repeat the rules—they were able to say why these rules are important for them. The children wanted to participate in the lesson and could hardly wait for their turns to be allowed to demonstrate good and bad school bus behavior. When I was a rookie with the state police and had to do those school assemblies on bicycle safety, I wondered how much of it would 'stick.' Acting out the rules did stay with them. The children listened to one another, too."

As Jason's experience illustrates, effective listening can make a real difference when it comes to recognizing danger, making wise decisions, and reacting appropriately.

3. Listening to appreciate, enjoy, and develop attitudes and values

Another important function of listening is to cultivate appreciation, enjoyment, and positive attitudes and values. Take, for example, the goal of respecting and appreciating different cultures. Rosa is a preschool teacher near Washington, DC. The 15 students in her class of 3- to 5-year-olds speak six different languages and represent seven different nationalities. From her study of creativity and the arts, Rosa

continued on p. 28

Using a "Mystery Object" Game to Develop Children's Thinking Skills

by Audrey C. Rule, Kathleen M. Lea, and Patricia A. Smith

We asked preschoolers (ages 3–5) at our college child care center to guess what mystery object we had hidden in a fabric-covered cracker box. They demonstrated several kinds of listening and thinking difficulties, and we devised ways to help them improve their skills, including attention, listening comprehension, and recall.

Children often repeated questions, even questions that had already received a negative answer:

> **Cole:** Is it blue?
> **Teacher:** No, not blue.
> **Maddy:** Is it yellow?
> **Teacher:** No, not yellow.
> **Aidan:** Is it blue?

Many of these children, absorbed in their own guesses and ideas, likely were not attending to the others' responses. We helped them notice the utility of listening to other children's questions by reviewing periodically what they knew about the mystery object and noting which questions had helped them know that.

Children usually started with specific guesses. A better game strategy is to ask general questions to determine a broad category, and then narrow the category until specific guesses identify the object. To help children learn this, a teacher modeled asking broader questions:

> **Second Teacher:** Is it something you color with?
> **Teacher:** Yes.
> **Second Teacher** (pointing to a desk): Can I use it at this desk?
> **Teacher:** Yes.

Many children seemed to have trouble determining what items were included in a category. Sometimes children had difficulty understanding what was meant when an item was *not* in a category. Although they were listening, young children typically remember verbatim information; they gradually learn, with additional experience and maturity, to attend to semantic or relational information (Courage & Howe 2004). They may also have difficulty conceptualizing negative statements (e.g., *"Not* a toy")—all things that make the Mystery Object activity intellectually challenging. For example,

> **Gabriel:** Is it a shirt?
> **Teacher:** No, it's not something you wear.
> **Zeida:** Is it a dress?

We determined that the children understood what it meant to *not* be included in a category. So we thought the problem might be that they struggled with the complexity of both thinking of things not in a category just mentioned and generating ideas of things not visually present. We wondered if playing classification games immediately before the Mystery Object game would help children formulate more general category questions or guess items that belonged to a determined category. We laid out two sets of items: (1) plate, cup, fork, spoon, and (2) doll, puppet, block, truck. Then we asked children to name the two categories, which they were able to do: "things to play with" and "things to cook with." This practice and the visual reminder of having items grouped into categories when devising questions seemed to help:

> **Teacher:** Remember; let's try to think of questions about the group it belongs to so we will have a clue.
> **Andrew:** Is it for cooking?
> **Teacher:** No, but that is a good question. Now we know it is not something you cook with, so we don't have to think about those things.
> **Sammy:** Is it a toy you play with?

After just two weeks of practice, playing the game twice a day, the children showed progress in determining a general category, sometimes narrowing the category, and in making appropriate guesses within that category. For example,

> **Teacher** (referring to grouped objects in front of the children): Remember we talked about why these things are alike. Do you think you can figure out what is in this box by asking a question about what group the thing would be in?
> **Sammy:** Do you cook with it?
> **Teacher:** Yes, that's a great question. Now think of things you can cook with.
> **Teddy:** Is it a spatula?
> **Teacher:** No, you can cook with a spatula, but this is a different thing you can cook with.
> **Sammy:** Is it a spoon?
> **Teacher:** No, not a spoon, but it is like a spoon.
> **Sammy:** Can you eat with it?
> **Teacher:** Yes, you eat with it. What do you think it is?
> **Sammy:** Do you stir your coffee with it?
> **Teacher:** You usually stir your coffee with a spoon, but this is not a spoon. What else do you eat with that is not a spoon?
> **Teddy:** A fork!
> **Teacher:** Yes! It is a fork!

Young children learn concretely by doing—feeling, touching, exploring. After they build this foundation, they can learn by listening, recalling, and processing those experiences mentally.

Audrey Rule is a professor in the Department of Curriculum and Instruction, and Kathleen Lea and Patricia Smith are teachers at the Children's Center of Oswego, at the State University of New York at Oswego.

sketches out the following listening activities to support the goal of promoting antibias in her curriculum:

- Invite families to loan or create recordings from their cultures and countries. Research simple folk dances or games that accompany musical selections to teach to children. Make arrangements for live performances of different musical instruments. For example, a parent from Nigeria will teach a song using the thumb piano.

- Check out culturally diverse materials from the library or children's museum that can be used at the classroom listening station or learning center. Connect these materials with curricular themes.

- Establish interdisciplinary collaborations with colleagues. For example, prepare a lesson on Appalachian music and culture that includes quilts, a dulcimer, an autoharp, and a demonstration of "musical" spoons. Let children experiment with moving a traditional wooden dancing doll "in time" to the music.

By combining arts integration and effective listening, a teacher can expand children's musical preferences and repertoires, deepen their appreciation for the arts in other cultures, engage diverse families and communities in the school curriculum, and promote the goals of multicultural education and inclusion.

Planning for active listening in the classroom

A first grade teacher confided, "After hearing myself repeat directions three, four, and maybe more times, I have decided that I need some help. I wish there was a magic wand, so that with one wave my students would listen and comply." Surely every teacher has, at one time or another, wished for silent, rapt attention. (About the only sure way to achieve complete quiet is to teach a televised or online course, where the students are virtual rather than real.) More than four decades ago, Sylvia Ashton Warner (1963) reminded us that children are "noisy creatures," and those who cannot tolerate the sounds of children should consider a different occupation (104).

Still, there is little question that even young children are expected to spend the majority of their classroom time listening. Even in

What We Know about the Arts and Listening

Listening is an important component of the arts. Young children listen to songs, stories, poetry, and drama long before they can perform in any of these realms.

- Young children's musical preferences often are established by age 8 (Isenberg & Jalongo 2007).

- Preschool children need to listen to music with attention and understanding as preparation for meeting K–4 arts standards and to set the foundation for a lifelong enjoyment of music (Music Educators National Conference 1994).

- Most young children have little opportunity to listen to recorded music for sustained periods of time, except in the background during naptime or playtime. They need practice learning to listen attentively to live and recorded music (Sims 2005).

- Anyone capable of hearing can hear the sounds of music. But listening actively to music—with focus, intent, and understanding—is both a talent and a skill, developed through modeling and practice (Copland 1996; Johnson & Koga 2006/2007).

- Children's ability to listen attentively to music varies enormously and does not appear to be related to gender, familiarity with the selection, or whether the music is vocal or instrumental. In a series of studies over 15 years, children listened to a musical selection for as few as 5 seconds and as much as almost 20 minutes (Sims 2005).

- Compared with sitting still with hands folded, "whole body" listening (e.g., moving hands in response to music) leads to greater levels of on-task behavior during music-related small group activities (Sims 2005; Truesdale 1990).

more interactive classrooms, "students' ability to engage, listen, and respond are still important determinants of both communicative and academic success" (Lapadat 2002, 278). Everyone agrees that children must be able to listen to succeed as learners, and that it is the teacher's role to help them learn to listen. The question, then, is how.

Think of a listening activity. If you are like most teachers, you might suggest giving children a set of verbal directions to follow, playing a game of Simon Says, making a tape of common household or classroom sounds for them to identify, or playing recordings of literature or music. But learning to listen needs to move well beyond such commonplace activities. That's where *active listening* comes into the classroom picture.

As described in the previous chapter, *effective listening* means the listener takes in the message accurately and interprets it appropriately. In *active listening,* the listener not only gets the message right but also uses an understanding of the message to become an active participant. For example, you could listen effectively to a book on tape while riding in your car—that is, you could hear the narration, focus on what you were hearing, and understand the storyline. But to participate fully in a discussion group about the book you would need to be an active listener—meaning you would act upon what you had heard, construct your own meaning, relate it to your life, and engage in the discussion with others.

Active listening is "listening between the lines," and can be done in much the same way as "reading between the lines." A situation that arose in a first grade classroom helps to illustrate active listening. Children were taking turns in the author's chair sharing their original picture books with their teacher and classmates. A child who was new to the classroom community shared the story of a lonely little rabbit who searched for (and finally found) a friend. When the story was finished, one of the children said quietly, "I liked your story and I was thinking that maybe you could come to my house to play sometimes." This child's poignant response offered evidence that she had understood not only her new classmate's written words but also had glimpsed the feelings below the surface. As demonstrated in this example, listening actively meant that the discussion mattered to the children. We all have an easier time absorbing things that matter to us, making us more engaged and interested learners.

As a first step in promoting *active listening* by children in their classrooms, teachers need to accept and model its basic principles (Brown 1991):

• Teaching and learning can occur without teacher talk.

- The emphasis should be on the listening/thinking connection rather than just hearing information.
- Children should play a major role in formulating questions.
- The teacher should probe deeper when an intriguing idea is raised.
- Children need to relate subject matter to their personal lives.
- Children should spend as much time listening to one another as to the teacher.
- Problems and conflicts often can be resolved by listening and talking together.

Making listening the emphasis

To emphasize listening and to make information more accessible, teachers should: (1) assess prior knowledge; (2) set a purpose for listening; (3) consider the structure of messages; (4) create a listening environment; (5) engage learners with the message; and (6) hold children accountable for listening.

1. Assess prior knowledge

Children rely on what they already know to understand what they do not yet know, often with surprising or humorous results.

> Four-year-old Tiffani's bedroom window was broken by a stray baseball. Her dad covered the hole with newspaper and masking tape until the pane could be replaced. When he finished, he told her, "There. Now no drafts will come in." A few minutes later he heard Tiffani crying, came back to her room, and asked her what was wrong. She answered, "Don't want no giraffes comin' in my window at night when I'm sleeping."

It probably would not occur to most adults that the word *drafts* could be mistaken for *giraffes*—but that is exactly what happened here to the zoo-savvy Tiffani. Children do rely on what they already know as they try to make sense out of the unfamiliar.

In early childhood settings, where individual children may be at very different levels of understanding spoken and written language, assessing prior knowledge and checking for understanding are essential to ensure listening comprehension.

2. Set a purpose for listening

This teacher used several strategies: "We will be making our puppets today, and there are three things you must remember...." After the teacher concluded his instructions, he asked the children to recall the three key points, and he wrote what they said on the board, thus reinforcing an auditory message (the three steps) with a visual one. Both giving clear instructions and supporting good listening habits should be part of the normal operating procedure in a classroom and should cut across all subject matter boundaries. Here are some additional suggestions for "weaving in" listening throughout the day (Plourde 1989):

- **Give instructions once, then encourage children to ask specific questions.** Teachers commonly complain that children do not follow instructions. The solution is not to keep repeating the same instructions but to switch from *one-way communication* to *two-way communication*. If we give instructions once and then invite questions, it prompts children to interact with the message. We become more lucid and concise in our explanations (we hope), and children are encouraged to practice active listening skills.

- **Throw children a "vocabulary curve."** Instead of always using familiar words, build children's vocabulary and listening skills by using new words in context. For example, after conducting a survey of second-graders' pets and making a simple bar graph to represent the data, a teacher might put children into small groups by announcing, "All the *feline* owners line up ... now all the *rodent* owners...." Using new vocabulary in context helps children remember it.

- **Use open-ended questions.** The best questions to ask children are those to which teachers do not have ready answers (Hendrick & Weissman 2005). For instance, if discussing the folk tale *The Little Red Hen*, teachers can ask what the hen did first, next, last (planted wheat, harvested it, made it into bread) as a check on literal understanding. These are "right there in the book" answers. But if teachers say to children, "Remember that the animals said, 'Not I!' to everything—planting seeds, harvesting the wheat, and making the bread—but when she asked, 'Who will help me eat the bread?' they all said, 'I will!' ... Why?" When questioned in this way, children are more likely to offer different answers and express their ideas in unique ways.

- **Engage children in group work.** Instead of having children work in quiet isolation, have them work together in many different groups to accomplish various tasks. Because the success of these groups depends on listening—to both the teacher and group members—children will need specific directions and supervised practice in fulfilling their roles. For example, as part of a science unit, first-graders were working on an anti-litter campaign. In groups of three, they designed posters to remind everyone to keep the school building and grounds clean. Before beginning, their teacher gave them five minutes to discuss their ideas while he moved from group to group and provided guidance. Then he told the class that each child would take on one of three different roles. He had pasted clip art on index cards to identify the three different roles: there needed to be someone to do the lettering (an image of a child writing), someone to do the illustration (an image of a child drawing a picture), and someone to put up the poster (an image of a roll of tape).

- **Increase student responsibility.** When we put children in charge of greeting classroom visitors, guiding classroom tours, making announcements, conducting interviews, and the like, we encourage them to listen carefully so they can assume these responsibilities with confidence. In turn, they experience what it feels like to have people listen to them.

3. Consider the structure of messages

If we familiarize children with many types of messages and present these messages using a variety of structures, they can become better listeners. As teachers consider the message structures they use, their directions also become clearer. There are five basic structural patterns in messages (Wyatt 1989) and giving children practice with each type of message builds their listening skills:

Procedural information explains how to do something in a step-by-step fashion. Suppose that children are going to plant a lima bean seed. The teacher could set the children's expectations as follows:

> "Today we are going to plant our bean seeds. I will tell you what to do first, next, and last. The first step is to put the soil into the cup. Just use one scoop of soil and try not to spill it. The next step is to plant the bean seed. Make a little hole with your finger, like this, and gently put the seed in there. Cover the hole with soil. The last thing to do is to water it. We are going to use an eyedropper to water the seed. You need to place it in the water and squeeze. Look what happens inside when I stop squeezing—right, it fills up with water. Now hold it over the seed and squeeze the top again, and the water comes out."

She could draw a picture of each step and label the pictures by number. Finally, the teacher could say, "Let's go over the steps again together. Then I will call your name, and you'll go back one at a time to plant your seed with our grandparent volunteer." With this activity, children learn how to listen to directions, understand the logic behind the procedure, and put the directions into practice.

Chronological information is arranged by temporal sequences or relationships. For example, a teacher began by reading children the poem "The End" in *Now We Are Six*, by A.A. Milne, the author of the *Winnie the Pooh* books:

> When I was One,
> I had just begun.
>
> When I was Two,
> I was nearly new.
>
> When I was Three,
> I was hardly Me.
>
> When I was Four,
> I was not much more.
>
> When I was Five,
> I was just alive.
>
> But now I am Six, I'm as clever as clever.
>
> So I think I'll be six now for ever and ever.

She then invited the children to think about things they could not do previously but now could do, following the pattern in the poem. One child wrote, "When I was 4, I used to need help to get Popsicles out of the freezer; but now that I am 6, I can get them all by myself." Listening to the poem and then relating it to themselves in a similar structure helped children understand chronological information. After several such exercises, they had an easier time comprehending other messages that used this structure.

Categorical information classifies things based on one or more common attributes. When children know that they will be asked to produce sets of things, it helps to focus their attention. For example, first-grader Ann was very excited about a game that her substitute teacher taught them called Category. With all of the children seated at their desks, the teacher announces: "Category: Names of zoo animals." The children then slap their desktops twice in unison, then clap twice in unison. Then the next child takes a turn calling out the name of a zoo animal:

> **Child 1:** Tiger!
>
> **All:** (Slap, slap, clap, clap)
>
> **Child 2:** Rhinoceros!
>
> **All:** (Slap, slap, clap, clap)
>
> **Child 3:** Zebra!

The game continues in this way until the children can no longer think of names for that category; then the teacher changes to a different category, such as farm animals, names of months, or toys. As the children grow more skilled with the game, the categories become more challenging—such as types of transportation, names of states, names of carnivores, and so forth. As children listen to one another, their vocabulary grows. One child might offer "tricycle" as the name of a toy, something that another child had not considered. As children listen to answers and get more creative, the game can go on longer—and their thinking, vocabulary, and listening skills improve.

A **comparative structure** uses similarities or differences to organize. For example, a kindergarten or first grade teacher might have students listen to decide whether or not certain words have similar sounds. This is the most basic skill involved in phonological awareness; if they cannot hear the difference in sounds, they cannot begin to manipulate sounds to form new words. Following the typical developmental trajectory, the activity would start with initial sounds (e.g., *cat/mat*), then final sounds (*cat/cap*), then middle sounds (*cat/cut*).

Causative messages explain *how* and *why* by presenting causes and effects. For example, guiding children to create "if, then" statements is a way to support children's thinking about messages with a causative structure. A teacher might ask questions such as, "If we leave the lid off the paste, then what will happen?" or, "If we forget to put on a paint smock, then what might happen?" When children know the reasons underlying classroom procedures, they are more likely to remember the procedures themselves. This is true for other types of information presented in this format.

Familiarizing children with the structure of messages sets their expectations and allows them to listen more attentively and effectively to the important messages within these different structures.

4. Create a listening environment

When the teacher focuses children's attention, piques their curiosity, minimizes distractions, and plans effective transitions from one type of activity to another, she is promoting better listening habits. For example, this student teacher completing her practicum in a first grade classroom was finding that her biggest challenge was getting children quiet and ready to work after a transition. After several weeks of a new routine, her problem was resolved:

> At first, the student teacher's only ideas were to try the things she remembered her teachers doing back when she was in elementary school—blinking the lights, awarding stickers to children who sat in their seats, or listing the names of children who misbehaved on the board. This wasn't working very well. Her supervisor suggested she plan something intriguing to grab the children's attention as soon as they came in the room from outside or finished their snacks.

> In response, she showed a starfish, a seahorse, a sand dollar, and a large shell during a study of sea creatures. At other times she focused the children's attention with an interesting photograph, a brain teaser, or other object children had not seen before. Each time she would say calmly, "We will begin as soon as everyone is quiet and ready to listen."

5. Engage learners with the message

If children are invested in listening and are given a fun way to engage with the message, they will be more attentive and take more out of the experience. On the first day of sharing a new Big Book, a teacher takes the children on a "picture walk" through the story. She invites them to make predictions about the story based on the illustrations and lists each prediction with the child's name next to it on the whiteboard. Guessing what the story might be about prior to hearing it read engages the learners. They want to know if they were right and, as a result, they listen more carefully and become more involved in the story. As the story progresses, she gives them opportunities to revise their predictions, further supporting their engagement in the message that they hear. The teacher also points out places where a phrase repeats, and children can join in as she reads—yet another way to sustain attention.

6. Hold children accountable for listening

Children will make more of an effort to listen carefully if they know they will use the information they hear in some way, especially if their listening leads to a motivating outcome. They should be asked to put what they have learned from listening to immediate use. Accountability is reinforced when we ask children to restate ("Repeat the steps in this experiment"), summarize ("What did you find out?"), reflect ("How will you do this all by yourself?"), and teach ("Levi was out yesterday; Cara, please show him what we did with the Cuisenaire rods").

Activities like the following one support children with different listening skills and strengths—in focusing attention, understanding new information, applying new learning, and appreciating what they hear. Think about how these children are held accountable for listening:

> Students from the high school band have come to visit the Head Start class in Room 2. The band members will be demonstrating the sounds played by each of their instruments. Before they begin, Ms. Lee tells the children that afterwards they are going to sing a new version of "Old MacDonald Had a Farm"—except their song will be "Room 2 Children Had a Band" and instead of animal names, they will be listing the names of the instruments and imitating the sound that each one makes. Excited by their getting to sing their special new song with band accompaniment, the children pay close attention to all the instruments as they are played.

Listening as the Foundation for Language Development

Teachers of young children are under considerable pressure to accelerate young children's pre-reading and reading skills. What is frequently overlooked by those outside the field is that oral language—listening and speaking—is one of the best ways to support growth in reading and writing.

- Realize that language learning is both social and developmental; children must interact with more-competent language users in order to master language. Listening is an important skill to be acquired before learning to read.

- Acknowledge that every child's language or dialect is worthy of respect as a method of communication. Language and dialect reflect the identities, values, and experiences of the child's family and community.

- Treat children as if they are conversationalists, even if they are not talking yet. Children learn very early about how conversations work (taking turns, looking attentively, using facial expressions) as long as they observe and interact with conversing adults. Studies show that even newborns engage in a sort of conversational "dance" with their caregivers, mimicking the interactions of a verbal conversation (Nelson 2007).

- Be sure to speak to *all* children, not just those capable of more advanced speech. Children need to be treated as competent language learners in order to develop language skills.

- Appreciate that if a child feels isolated or marginalized, listening can help us to identify with the child's feelings (Messiou 2006). Hearing a child say, "My grandma had chemo today. Now all her hair fell out," helps the teacher to be more compassionate.

- Ask children to talk about things that truly matter to *them,* such as what they want to learn or what they like best about school. When teachers "follow the child's agenda" (rather than fire off questions that elicit parroted-back answers) it puts us back in touch with the reasons we went into teaching in the first place. Children's comments sometimes leave us without words, as when a child asked, "Why aren't you supposed to walk on a grave? Is it because they can feel it?"

- Design activities that encourage children to listen to one another carefully. Listening to and learning from peers are important to language and social development. Listening to a peer with a language delay or disorder, to an English language learner, or during the intense negotiations that often accompany play enables the child to become more versatile, adept, and sensitive as a listener.

Source: Based on Lu (2000).

Conclusion

We know from listening research that there is a direct relationship between listening and learning, but that good listening does not occur automatically. Listening skills can be taught, and listening needs to be part of the total curriculum. To become good listeners, young children need to do more than just "put on your listening ears"; they need to participate in challenging, meaningful listening activities that develop their listening abilities. The best way teachers can help children to become better listeners is to stop thinking of *listening* as a synonym for "hearing" or even for "understanding what is heard." Instead, we need to think of listening as the foundation for language development.

Chapter 3

Meeting the Diverse Needs of Young Listeners

Listening is one of the primary methods by which children acquire the beliefs, norms, and knowledge bases of their society.

—Teresa McDevitt

Although we can chart typical developmental milestones and identify general patterns of growth, each child progresses in his or her own way. Each uses the ability to listen in ways that are sometimes predictable and sometimes unexpected. For many young children, listening functions as a bridge between the familiar and the new. This is particularly true for English language learners. Language is one of the most important tools for social interaction, and acquiring English enables English language learners to participate more fully in society at large. Therefore, it is typical for children who are immersed in a new language environment to rely heavily on listening. They often go through a period of relative silence as they "take in" language and store it up before initial attempts to speak in the second language (Krashen 1988; 2003). Mei's story illustrates this point:

> When he first arrived at preschool, Mei, an English language learner, would not take off his jacket or come into the classroom. He stood on the threshold, hands thrust into his pockets, firmly refusing to step inside. The teacher brought him a chair and carried objects to him that

might capture his attention—such as a puppet, the class guinea pig, and a small toy truck—while naming each in English. Later that week, Mei agreed to play with sand and water and to put his jacket in the cubby. By the beginning of the next week, he sat at the table while the other children played with manipulatives. He joined in a picture lotto game and became very skilled at it.

But it was not until the third week that Mei began to use his new language beyond a few single-word utterances. The children gathered at circle time to sing a simple folk song. All of a sudden Mei smiled, sang the words in English, and clapped his hands with great enthusiasm. The other children were surprised and delighted by his participation.

Breakthroughs in a child's willingness to use expressive language (speaking) usually emanate from the accumulation of *comprehensible input*—spoken words that were made understandable through the additional efforts of adults and peers. Children learning English need teachers who will use the children's listening skills and strive to communicate with them. Juanita's situation, below, demonstrates the need for teachers to recognize an English language learner's period of relative silence as a precursor to expressive language:

Juanita was the 4-year-old daughter of migrant farm laborers from Mexico. Her parents enrolled her in a federally funded preschool program, which she attended while they were working. When Juanita first arrived, she clung to her mother and, although she did not cry, seemed a bit overwhelmed by all of the new faces, activities, materials, and the predominance of a language that she did not know. For the first three weeks, whenever something captivated her attention, Juanita responded with shy smiles and nods of appreciation, but still no words—in either Spanish or English.

After saying good-bye to her mother, Juanita's morning routine was to make a beeline for the preschool's child-sized kitchen. One bright summer morning, Juanita stood at the play stove, stirring a pot and singing an invented lullaby in Spanish to the doll she held on her hip. Sensing an opportunity, her teacher grabbed a plastic telephone and rang the bell on it. When Juanita picked up the other toy phone, her teacher greeted her in Spanish. Juanita replied, also in Spanish, that she was cooking dinner and the baby was crying. From that point forward, Juanita began speaking and participating. When the teacher invited the children to bring a snack for the class, Juanita and her mother volunteered to prepare one. Juanita rolled out perfectly shaped tortillas, and after her mother flipped them into an electric frying pan, she distributed them to her eager, interested classmates.

As Juanita's story suggests, listening affects development across all areas of the curriculum and can influence many important functions, including motor skills, visual processing, auditory processing, attention, and speech and language (Brigman, Lane, & Switzer 2001). Juanita relied on her previous listening experiences (when she listened to someone sing a lullaby to a baby) and linked that listening to her dramatic play (rocking a doll while singing to it); she used her knowledge of conversations to respond to the bell and listen to her teacher's message on the plastic telephone; and she comprehended and conveyed to her mom the teacher's invitation to prepare a snack. The teacher in this situation recognized the skills that Juanita did have and used them to develop both her language and her confidence.

The role of listening in language development

Listening is the first of the five senses to mature. Listening also is where language development begins. The four "traditional" areas of the language arts are listening, speaking, reading, and writing. The chart on the next page shows the relationships among them. Note that listening is directly linked to reading, because both are receptive language arts, requiring the receiver to interpret a message. Listening is so fundamental that children who have listening comprehension problems usually have problems with speaking, reading, and writing, as well.

Most teachers are familiar with the time-honored strategy of beginning "where children are" and using developmentally effective practice. What better way to introduce speaking, reading, and writing, then, than with the ability that most children develop even before birth: listening (Jalongo 2006). Consider how the listening behavior of these children illustrates the progression from listening, to speaking, to reading and writing:

- A fussy newborn grows calm and quiet as he hears his grandmother's voice singing a lullaby that is part of their shared cultural heritage. Within a few months the baby begins to vocalize when he hears those familiar songs.

- A toddler hears the meowing of the family cat, which has accidentally been trapped inside a bedroom closet. As the child

Listening as One of the Four Language Arts

	Oral Language– relies on spoken words	Text-Based Language– relies on print materials
Receptive– receives and interprets a message	**Listening** • Usually begins at birth to 1 year • Children learn to make sense out of the messages they hear	**Reading** • Typically begins near age 5 • Children use oral language to decipher written language
Expressive– composes and transmits a message	**Speaking** • Often begins near the end of the first year • Children use language to express their ideas	**Writing** • Ordinarily begins near age 6 • Children use knowledge of oral language and printed words to express their ideas

Source: Minskoff (2005).

slides open the door to set it free, she announces proudly, "kee-kot," her toddler version of the words *kitty cat*. She has used her sense of hearing to interpret and solve a problem.

- A group of children in a public preschool program have heard the book *Down by the Cool of the Pool* many times. When their teacher reads the Big Book version aloud, they listen for their cue and chime in on parts that they know well.

- A kindergarten child uses an assistive communication device to interact with his peers. The communication panel has a variety of images on large buttons that, when pressed, make a computer-generated voice speak the word for each image. The other children are fascinated by this way of communicating and urge their classmate on: "Make it say something else" … "Ask me a question."

- A second-grader practices her reading skills by listening to an electronic "talking" book on the computer. As she watches the animation and follows along with the highlighted text, a digitized voice reads each word aloud. She clicks on unfamiliar words to hear them pronounced again and defined. Later, when she reads with a tutor, her practice enables her to read the book with greater confidence and fluency.

Problems with listening are often major obstacles in acquiring literacy with print. In one study, some 50 percent of the children observed who had reading disabilities also had significantly lower scores on oral language (listening, speaking) measures than their peers did, demonstrating a link between oral and written language skills (Heath & Hogben 2004). Early reading difficulties are often linked to problems with listening. In fact, the most common cause of early reading difficulties is weakness in children's ability to apprehend, manipulate, and use the sound structure of spoken language (Minskoff 2005). Even the major reading disability, dyslexia, usually is attributed to an inability to master the sound system of language, or the *phonology*. Problems with oral language frequently lead to academic difficulties:

> Children with receptive and/or expressive language difficulties will likely struggle in school because they cannot easily learn under typical classroom conditions. These children cannot always keep up with the pace of verbal instruction, they may not consistently understand the content of ideas being discussed, and they may not have strong skills for communicating what they do or do not know. As a result, they may become withdrawn in school or appear inattentive because they lose their focus when they do not hear or understand what is being discussed. (Cruger 2005, 1)

Thus, problems with listening often are associated with low academic achievement—particularly in reading—and school failure. The chart beginning on the next page summarizes research on listening and young children, both with and without disabilities. As this developmental overview details, listening has a profound effect on literacy and overall academic achievement. Meeting the needs of diverse language learners requires attention to the many conditions and circumstances that interfere with effective listening, so that literacy and academic success are possible for all children.

What the Research Says about Young Children's Listening and Language Learning

Prebirth to 1 Year Old

• From the earliest days of life, the sense of hearing is fully formed and functioning. Even within the womb, as soon as the hearing organs are fully developed, the fetus is capable of hearing. A fetus attends to the mother's voice and can distinguish it from the voices of other women (DeCasper et al. 1994).

• Newborns are sensitive to pitch (Saffran & Griepentrog 2001).

• Newborns suck more rapidly when they are interested in something. When speech and other sounds are played, newborns suck more rapidly in response to language. This demonstrates a preference for speech (Vouloumanos & Werker 2007).

• Infants respond to the primary caregiver's voice and can distinguish between the language spoken by their mother and other languages (Mehler & Dupoux 1994).

• Most babies are born with the ability to perceive *phonemes,* the smallest units of meaningful sound. Even a 4-week-old baby can detect the difference between the letter sounds of *g* and *k,* for example (Richgels 2001).

• Listening affects mood. Infants on respirators breathe more rhythmically when music with a strong beat, rather than a lullaby, is played softly in the background (Bayless & Ramsey 1990).

• Five-month-olds pay more attention to their own names than to similar-sounding words (Jusczyk 2000).

• Caregivers often use *child-directed speech* (CDS) when interacting with infants. CDS consists of dramatic facial expressions and gestures (such as eyes open wide with eyebrows raised in surprise), slow and simple speech, and emphasized key words through tone of voice (Nelson 2007). Studies show that infants pay attention better when caregivers use child-directed speech (Kratcoski & Katz 1998).

• *Vocal imitation* is one of the earliest communicative strategies used by children. It is positively correlated with language learning, length of utterances, spontaneous speech, and acquisition of new vocabulary and grammatical structures (Gazdag & Warren 2000).

• At 6 to 8 months, American infants sound pretty much like infants from other cultures, babbling and cooing. Even congenitally deaf infants babble, although less frequently than their hearing peers (DeVilliers 1990).

• Newborns are able to distinguish the sounds of all languages. But by 6 months of age, they have pruned their listening down to the sounds of their native tongue (Shiver 2002).

• By 8 months, infants are tuned into the phonetic properties of their native tongue and no longer respond to phoneme distinctions that are not part of their own language (Jusczyk 2000).

1 to 3 Years Old

• Toddlers use repetitive pointing and pantomime as important communication tools (Goodwin & Accredolo 2000).

• A toddler's *receptive* vocabulary—the words he can understand—is often as much as four times greater than his *expressive* vocabulary—the words he can produce (Griffiths 1986).

• Toddlers learn to interpret what another is talking about—even if an object referred to is out of sight (Tomasello 2003).

• In a study of toddlers (with and without a hearing loss), there was a positive relationship between the number of words produced and the amount of time spent on pretend play (Brown, Rickards, & Bortoli 2001).

• By about 15 months, many toddlers have an oral vocabulary (speaking) of about 10 words (Nelson 2007).

• Eighteen-month-olds often can tell from the context what word the speaker is going to say, after hearing the first two phonemes (e.g., from "Where's your te…?" the child understands that the adult is asking where his *teddy bear* is) (Fernald, Swingley, & Pinto 2001).

• By 16 months, most toddlers can understand simple requests. By 19 months, some advanced children comprehend about 100 words and phrases (Nelson 2007).

• By age 2 most children have a speaking vocabulary of about 50 words and are beginning to grasp abstract concepts such as "another" and "more" (Thal & Flores 2001; Nelson 2007).

• At the end of the second year, most children know between 50 and several hundred words and have begun making two- and three-word combinations. They often learn one to two new words per week (Nelson 2007).

• Some 97 percent of 3-year-olds can connect two to three words to form phrases and simple sentences. Most have also begun to listen to word order as a way to help them interpret sentences (Thal & Flores 2001).

• Listening requires the ability to pay attention. When parents were asked to compare their children with their peers, 13 percent rated their child as "attending less well" or "much less well" than others in the same age group. Boys were identified twice as often as girls as having deficiencies in attention and articulation (National Research Council 2001).

continued on p. 48

3 to 8 Years Old

• Listening is the foundation for speaking, reading, and writing in children without hearing impairments (Isbell et al. 2004; Nation & Snowling 2004).

• Around age 3 it is common for children to engage in bedtime monologues during which they experiment aloud with the sounds and words that they have heard throughout the day (Nelson 2007).

• By age 5 a child's receptive vocabulary soars to nearly 8,000 words. It is estimated that preschoolers learn 6 to 10 new words a day (Tabors & Snow 2001).

• Readers and prereaders listen differently. Prereaders have significantly shorter memory spans and are more tuned into meaning than individual sounds (Nelson 2007).

• Oral language deficits often are connected with attention deficit and hyperactivity disorder (ADHD) (McInnes et al. 2003).

• About 3 percent of children from 6 to 11 years of age are diagnosed with ADHD, and 4 percent are diagnosed with learning disabilities (Minskoff 2005).

• It is estimated that a child needs a vocabulary of about 8,000 to 9,000 words in order to independently read and understand text; in order to independently understand spoken language and engage in fluent conversation, the vocabulary demands are somewhat smaller—about 6,000 to 7,000 words (Nation 2006).

• The relationship between listening comprehension and reading comprehension gets stronger as children's word recognition becomes increasingly automatic (Crain-Thorenson 1996).

• Children's overall oral language proficiency (listening, speaking), as well as their phonological skills, influences the course of reading development (Nation & Snowling 2004).

• Children with average or above average oral language and above average phonological short-term memory are far more likely to become good readers (Heath & Hogben 2004).

• Children can detect sounds of language before they can blend, manipulate, or segment sounds. They first master word-level sounds, then syllable-level skills, then initial consonants and "sounding out" all the parts of a word (Anthony & Lonigan 2004).

• By the spring of first grade, almost all children recognize their letters, 98 percent of children understand beginning sounds, 94 percent understand ending sounds, and 83 percent recognize very common words by sight (National Center for Education Statistics 2002).

• Children with ADHD may comprehend surface details adequately, but may show deficits on more challenging tasks that require more persistence (McInnes et al. 2003).

Learning to Listen, Listening to Learn

Obstacles to listening

There are four broad categories of obstacles to effective listening in the classroom: (1) physiological, (2) cognitive and language processing, (3) psychological, and (4) issues with experience, skills, and training.

Physiological obstacles

Permanent, irreversible, and significant hearing loss or impairment is the most formidable obstacle to listening. About 50 percent of severe hearing loss is thought to be genetic (McCormick, Loeb, & Schiefelbusch 2002); but other causes are injury and illness. By coincidence, both boys in the following vignette had *sensorineural* hearing loss, a dysfunction in the inner ear, auditory nerve, or neural pathway. A sound signal may arrive in the brain in a highly distorted form, or maybe not at all.

> A kindergarten teacher had two boys with hearing impairments in her class and a full-time interpreter who used American Sign Language to communicate with them. One day when the boys were out of the room, she asked their classmates if they had any questions about hearing loss. Some of their questions were:
>
> "When did they get deaf?"
>
> "How do you know what Timmy and Chris are saying?"
>
> "Do they live in the same house?"
>
> "When will they learn to talk?"

As their questions suggest, the children assumed that because the boys could communicate with each other, they were related, and that their hearing impairments were reversible. In fact, even with amplification, the sound impulses would remain unclear, and medical and surgical procedures are of limited usefulness in cases of sensorineural hearing loss (McCormick, Loeb, & Schiefelbusch 2002).

But not every child with a physiological obstacle to listening has a loss so significant, although misconceptions about children with hearing loss are common (Marschark 2007). There are degrees of hearing loss, and many hearing-impaired children have some residual hearing (Easterbrooks & Estes 2007). Some children who are deaf can hear certain pitches at particular decibel levels. Technological advances in hearing aids and other assistive devices can sometimes capitalize on these capabilities.

In fact, physiological impediments to listening are not that rare. Approximately 28 million Americans have hearing loss (ASHA 2007a) and about one in every 40 students has a communication disorder serious enough to warrant speech therapy or other special education services (Slavin 2005). Within the K–12 population, 13 out of every 1,000 have some degree of hearing loss (ASHA 2004).

Some types of hearing loss or impairment are temporary, rather than permanent and irreversible. Temporary fluctuations in hearing can be caused by illness (e.g., stuffy ears from a cold), prescription drug side effects, injuries, or poor hygiene (e.g., a build-up of ear-wax). Other types of hearing loss are chronic but treatable (e.g., from allergies). Ear infections, for example, are one of the most common childhood illnesses:

- More than two-thirds of all children get an ear infection before they turn 3. Every year, half of all children under 5 will experience at least one ear infection (Hearing, Speech, and Deafness Center 2007).

- Children who suffer extended periods of hearing loss due to recurrent ear infections score lower on speech and language tests administered at age 3 than do children with little or no history of ear infections (Hearing, Speech, and Deafness Center 2007).

A typical example is Caitlin, a first-grader with a history of ear infections who has taken several courses of antibiotics during her young life. She has fluid in her ears from the infections, and the side effects of the drugs are tinnitus (ringing in her ears) and drowsiness.

> In the spring semester of first grade, Caitlin developed tonsillitis. Her parents decided to wait until summertime to schedule a tonsillectomy so she would not miss school. Because of the fluid and ringing in her ears, the sounds she hears are distorted. This makes it difficult for her to accurately hear and produce the sounds of language. Phonics is a major component of the first grade reading instruction at her school, and Caitlin is experiencing difficulty learning to read.

Due to the prevalence of conditions such as Caitlin's, it is estimated that on any given day up to one-third of kindergarten and first grade students are not hearing as well as they should be (Flexer 1997).

Teachers can do a lot to support children with physiological problems that affect listening. First among them is to help identify children who may have undiagnosed impairments by observing

---

Why Early Assessment and Intervention Is Important

Because the ability to hear is critical for the development of language communication skills and learning, early screening and intervention are essential. Evaluation of a child's hearing often does not occur until he or she enters kindergarten, which puts young children at very high risk for early learning problems associated with hearing difficulties.

- A child may be labeled as *unmotivated, inattentive,* or *lacking task persistence* when he really is experiencing undetected hearing problems (Cruger 2005).

- Families may think they have a particularly "good baby" if the child does not startle easily, when actually the child may have a hearing impairment (ASHA 2004; 2007a).

- Technology exists to assess hearing in children of all ages. Increasingly, hospitals are screening newborns (American Society for Deaf Children 2007).

- Babies taught to use American Sign Language early will master it more readily (ASHA 2004; 2007a).

- Infants as young as 4 weeks old can be fitted with hearing aids and other assistive devices (ASHA 2004; 2007a).

- Children with hearing impairments who begin services before they are 6 months old often show language development patterns comparable to their peers who don't have impairments (ASHA 2004; 2007a).

- Cochlear implants inserted early and supported with language activities in the home and regular intervention can enable young children to hear and function in society much like other children (Eisenberg, Fink, & Niparko 2006; Ertmer & Mellon 2001).

---

their classroom behavior. There can be other explanations, but it can be an indicator of hearing loss if a child:

- Frequently misunderstands what is said and asks for things to be repeated.

- Appears to have difficulty following verbal instructions and/or responds inconsistently.

- Often turns up the volume of the computer, CD/DVD player, or other recorded materials.

- Has speech and/or language problems that make it difficult for people outside the family to understand his speech.

- Has a short attention span or poor memory for sounds or words in comparison with her peers.

- Has reading, spelling, or other academic problems.

- Feels isolated, excluded, annoyed, embarrassed, confused, or helpless.

- Has a family history of hearing loss, chronic ear infections, and/or exposure to damaging levels of noise (ASHA 2004; 2007a).

If you suspect an impairment, the next step would be talking with the family and your program. A number of screenings and tests are available from hearing specialists to aid in diagnosis.

Other things we can do include checking the child's health records, learning as much as we can about resources available and making referrals, and educating ourselves about deaf culture. Some accommodations for children who have trouble hearing are simple, such as seating them close to you so they can lip read or hear better. A child with a significant degree of hearing impairment typically will have an IEP and other supports in place.

Cognitive and language processing obstacles

Cognitive conditions that commonly interfere with a child's ability to listen effectively include attentional difficulties, learning disabilities, language disorders, and language processing problems.

Children with attentional difficulties and learning disabilities frequently find it challenging to maintain focus.

Hearing Tests for Very Young Children

Test	What	How
Otoacoustic Emissions (OAE) Screening	A quick screening to check for the possibility of some degree of hearing loss; determines the necessity of further assessment. It can be used with infants.	*Otoacoustic emissions* are sounds produced by healthy ears in response to sound. The emissions result from activity of the outer hair cells in the inner ear. The child must be still. A small earpiece attached to a computer is inserted into each ear and a sound is transmitted. If the computer does not record an emission, the hair cells may not be working and the child may have a hearing loss.
Auditory Brainstem Response (ABR) Evaluation	A thorough test to determine the quietest sounds the ear can detect at a variety of pitches.	The child must be asleep and usually is sedated for this painless procedure, which can take an hour or more to complete. Electrodes are placed on the child's head and earphones are placed over the ears. The earphones transmit sounds, and the electrodes detect the brain's response to the sounds for each ear.
Behavioral Audiometry	Various tests to evaluate a child's response to a variety of sounds, such as speech or pure tones.	For infants, motions that suggest the infant has been startled by the sounds are observed. These physical reactions might include changes in body orientation, changes in the speed of sucking, widening of eyes, etc. Other tests in this category might condition an older child to respond to hearing a sound with a specific action; for example, responding by looking toward the sound, placing an object in a box, or stacking a ring on a stick.

Source: Based on American Society for Deaf Children (2007).

Shelby is a preschooler with attentional difficulties. He can hear perfectly well; but his focus breaks when interruptions occur, the teacher's voice rises and drops as she moves around the room, or background noise competes for his attention. Listening is a lot of work, and Shelby grows weary of struggling to listen and understand.

Early screening and intervention are essential because cognitive conditions that affect listening also interfere with children's development of language skills and learning. For example, 56 percent of students with learning disabilities have problems completing homework assignments; the problems often are attributable to poor receptive language (listening, reading) and memory deficits, both of which interfere with understanding or remembering what has been assigned (Bryan & Burstein 2004).

Children may also have language processing problems, which concern the way that messages are interpreted. One language processing problem that can greatly affect listening is called *auditory processing disorder* (APD). When a child does not appear to have a cognitive or attentional deficit yet seems to have difficulty getting the message, he may have problems processing the sounds from each ear simultaneously and filtering out noise (Jerger 2006).

Psychological obstacles

The ability to listen also can be impaired by distracting or upsetting factors such as fatigue, hunger, illness, or toileting needs. When children are under severe stress—such as when they are abused emotionally or physically—they are understandably preoccupied with that situation and may appear to be inattentive, distant, and withdrawn.

Contextual variables also exert an influence on listening. Children may "tune out" if they do not feel accepted by the speaker or if they are not interested in the message:

> Marta is an exuberant kindergartner who has come to the conclusion that her teacher does not like her very much. Once, when Marta reported that another child had taken her barrettes, the teacher responded, "Oh, I don't think so. Please sit down." Marta came home and asked, "What kind of teacher would let somebody take a little kid's barrettes?"
>
> On another occasion while the class was rehearsing for a musical performance, the teacher asked Marta and a few other children not to sing. The children were very upset; they knew they had been singled out because the teacher thought they did not sing well. When Marta's mother inquired about this during a conference, asking why her daughter was not allowed to sing, the teacher's response was, "'Singing' might be what you call it, but I wanted the class to sound *good*." Not long afterwards, Marta's parents were called in because their child was re-

portedly "not paying attention," and it was true. In fact, when questioned, Marta admitted, "Sometimes I look out the window when the teacher is talking. I know she doesn't like me, so why should I pay attention?"

Obstacles of experience, skills, and training

Experience, skills, and training affect listening, as well. This includes the child's interest in the message, perception of the speaker, and proficiency in the language. Anyone who has studied a second language knows that it takes a determined effort to make sense out of the messages that are heard, and that misunderstandings are commonplace. Adults studying another language are typically fluent in at least one language; they know its *phonology* (sound system), *semantics* (meaning system), *syntax* (structure or grammar), and *pragmatics* (uses in various social situations). However, very young children who are English language learners are still becoming proficient in their *first* language when the second language is introduced—making the situation even more difficult. These children are inexperienced not only as listeners but also as language learners in general.

Listening effectively in a new and unfamiliar language is a major challenge:

> Natasha, a second-grader from Russia, is now living in the southern United States. Although she had studied English a little, she now must contend with a completely different alphabet, deal with the rapid rate of speech and regional dialects in the South, and acquire a completely new vocabulary.

The box on the next page summarizes some key findings related to listening and second language learning.

Other challenges to listening are related to skills and training. Many young children hear normally and have no psychological or cognitive disabilities; they just haven't learned how to focus and concentrate in the presence of competing demands for their attention. Effective listening, like so many other skills, has to be taught and learned. While children spend about 58 percent of their classroom time listening, their teachers devote only about 8 percent of instruction time to actually *teaching* listening skills (Cramond 1998). Fortunately, there is compelling evidence that children (and adults) can improve their listening skills through training, and that even short-

Learning to Listen to English as a Second Language

As one of the four language arts, *listening* shares with *speaking*, *reading*, and *writing* many of the same developmental principles. It benefits similarly from effective English language learning pedagogy. Early childhood educators who work effectively with English language learners use listening as a scaffold for teaching the other three language arts:

- Hearing two languages spoken from birth enables a child to speak each with the accent of a native speaker (Napoli 2003).

- English language learners have more difficulty recognizing English words in noisy or reverberant conditions than do native English speakers (Rogers et al. 2006).

- When the English vocabulary used in the home is very limited, a child's receptive and expressive vocabulary in English is likewise restricted (Naudé, Pretorius, & Viljoen 2003).

- English language learners do not necessarily have proficiency in their home language. Preschoolers may possess smaller vocabularies in both the first and the second languages than do children whose only language is English (Tabors & Snow 2001).

- In the absence of strong support for their first language, children who are English language learners can lose their ability to communicate in it within two to three years after starting school (Cummins 2003).

- In situations where the child's home language is established, *effective* bilingual programs use that language as a support for teaching the child English (Napoli 2003). When children are denied support in their first language, it takes 7 to 10 years for children to reach age- and grade-level norms in English (Thomas & Collier 1997).

- Children seldom master English if their first language is ignored or eradicated (David et al. 2006).

term training can be effective in improving children's listening habits (Goh & Taib 2006; Nichols, Brown, & Keller 2006). Teachers also need to consider environmental variables that distract children from listening, such as room temperature and background noise.

Supporting listening in inclusive programs

The previous chapter described how we need to approach pedagogy and classroom management from a very different perspective in order to promote *active listening* by children in our classrooms. The first step was to accept and model active listening's basic principles. Here we continue that stage-setting thinking, specifically to meet the diverse needs of young listeners. A teacher has the best chance of supporting *all* children as listeners when her approach:

- Recognizes that different children pursue different paths in becoming effective listeners (Dockrell, Stuart, & King 2004; Wambacq et al. 2005).

- Establishes learning environments that respect children's cultures and linguistic diversity.

- Provides opportunities for all children to be heard, not only by the teacher but also by peers.

- Designs learning activities that enable children to construct meaning from multiple sources, including not only what they hear but also other modalities.

- Enriches and extends children's listening in a variety of contexts and situations.

- Connects listening activities to national and disciplinary standards.

What follows are five general approaches that can meet these criteria and are supported by the research.

1. Incorporate listening goals and standards

Curriculum and pedagogy exert major influences on children's listening behavior. As a first step, consider the listening and speaking goals of your program and compare them with national, state, and disciplinary standards. For example, at the national level, the U.S. Department of Education (2002) offers guidance to preschool teachers and caregivers on developing children's listening skills because "research shows beyond question that it is through having many opportunities to talk as well as to listen to teachers and peers that children gain language skills so valuable for their success in reading and writing."

Almost all states have their own academic standards that focus on listening; usually, they are part of the language arts standards to which every teacher is held accountable. Another source for comparison is the K–12 disciplinary standards from the National Communication Association (1998). All three kinds of listening standards are shown in the box *opposite*.

Early childhood curriculum commonly teaches "the senses." But study of the senses should go beyond the ear and hearing, to the mind and heart. We can encourage young children to connect listening with feelings and emotions. For example, children might sort pictures into two categories: things they like to hear and things they do not like to hear (Merkel-Piccini 2001). They could also put together class books with the titles *What We Like to Hear* and *What We Don't Like to Hear*, to which each child contributes a page of drawing or writing. Included in one first grade class' *What We Like to Hear* book were illustrations accompanying these dictated sentences:

> "I like to hear the sound of bacon frying in the morning."
>
> "I like to hear that we're going to grandma's."
>
> "I like to hear my mom sing at church."

Included in that class' *What We Don't Like to Hear* book were:

> "I don't like to hear 'It's time for bed.'"
>
> "I don't like to hear guns and sirens."
>
> "I don't like to hear my cousins say, 'You're too little to go.'"

Some fantastic illustrations on these topics have been reproduced in color in this book after Chapter 4.

National, State, and Disciplinary Standards for Listening

U.S. Department of Education (2002)

It is important for young children to be able to:

- Listen carefully for different purposes, such as to get information or for enjoyment
- Use spoken language for a variety of purposes
- Follow and give simple directions and instructions
- Ask and answer questions
- Use appropriate volume and speed when they speak
- Participate in discussions and follow the rules of polite conversation, such as staying on a topic and taking turns
- Use language to express and describe their feelings and ideas

Typical State Listening Standards for Kindergarten (Seefeldt 2005)

Children will:

- Identify sounds in their environment
- Create sounds by singing and other music making
- Listen and speak with attention
- Listen for pleasure
- Develop phonemic awareness
- Identify letter-sound relationships

National Communication Association's (1998) K–12 Listening Competencies

Competent listeners demonstrate:

- Knowledge and understanding of the listening process
- The ability to use appropriate and effective listening skills for a given communication situation and setting
- The ability to identify and manage barriers to listening

2. Build phonics skills

Listening is the foundation of learning to read, and mastery of the *phonology,* or sound system, of a language is an undeniable advantage in interpreting the printed word. It is a common misconception that working with the sound system of language is beyond the capabilities of young children. But, in fact, there are many ways that children can practice these skills. Basic phonics skills include: rhyming words, counting syllables, manipulating word families (by *onsets* and *rimes*), recognizing compound words, making and breaking words, segmenting sounds, and blending sounds (Gunning 1995; Minskoff 2005). Let's look at just the first one in more detail:

Rhyming involves both the ability to discriminate words that sound alike (a receptive task) and the ability to produce words that sound alike (an expressive task). A requisite skill children need first is an awareness of sounds (*"Bike,* that sounds like my name, Mike!"). Usually, they notice rhymes long before they are reading words or have the vocabulary to call them rhymes (*"Funny* and *bunny,* those words go together"). Activities that teach rhyming might be:

- Begin with picture words that rhyme and do not rhyme. Ask children which pairs "sound alike" or "go together" and which do not (e.g., *snake/cake, cat/moon, fox/box, book/cake*). After children have identified rhyming words reliably, teach them the word *rhyme.*

- Provide more practice, asking them to stand up when a word pair rhymes and sit down when it does not; or provide them with YES/NO response cards to hold up.

- Read aloud a story with numerous rhyming words. Exaggerate the rhyming words a bit as you read. Ask children to hold up an index finger when they hear the rhyme.

- Have children work with a partner to make books of words that rhyme.

- Create a self-correcting game in which pairs of rhyming words fit together like puzzle pieces so children can practice independently.

3. Increase vocabulary by reading aloud

One of the best predictors of learning to read is a child's knowledge of vocabulary (Cain & Oakhill 2006). *Oral vocabulary* is the mental storehouse of words a child recognizes when listening or uses when speaking. *Reading vocabulary* refers to words a child recognizes or uses in reading and writing (Armbruster, Lehr, & Osborn 2003).

Few activities are more associated with early childhood education than reading aloud. But we should not assume that young children are naturally skilled at listening to stories. In fact, there is some evidence that it is a more challenging listening comprehension task than we may have thought (Westene 1997). To fully understand what is read aloud to them, children need an ever-expanding vocabulary for the story's unfamiliar places, characters, and actions. They also need to consider the relationships in the story, use their working memory to link later sentences to previous ones, connect pictures with words, and grasp the point of the story.

Children can acquire new vocabulary as they listen to their teacher read aloud, particularly when the teacher uses interactive reading strategies. The most effective way we can expand a child's vocabulary is to elaborate on the words in the story as we read. A first grade class was captivated by the concept of a "favor" in the picture book *Wolf's Favor* (Testa). In this story, Wolf is approached by Porcupine, who asks Wolf to crack a nut for him. Wolf obliges, and Porcupine shares the nut with an animal friend, who helps out another friend, and so forth until the good will comes full circle and a favor is done for Wolf. Before the children listened to the story, the teacher asked them, "If someone says to you, 'Could you please do me a favor?' what does that mean?" Several children offered explanations, and as they discussed the concept of favors, the teacher emphasized that sometimes we do things to get a reward, but when it's a favor, we don't expect anything in return. After listening to the book, children spoke about favors in ways that demonstrated their understanding of the concept: "Would you do me a favor and help with this zipper on my coat?" or "Carlotta wanted to know how to spell *horse,* so I did her a favor and showed her." Encouragingly, children with the smallest vocabularies often make the greatest gains when we talk about the new words the child encounters in the book (Justice, Meier, & Walpole 2005).

4. Make the most of multiple modes

When we plan lessons that offer children ways to participate other than by just listening or just speaking (especially only in English), we give all the children an opportunity to listen and understand. For example:

> It is August and a first grade teacher is discussing the parts of plants with her class. Six of the 28 children are English language learners. She has prepared flannel board cutouts of the basic parts of a plant—flower, leaf, stem, root—and written the name of each part on a card. She places circles of yarn on the floor, one for each plant part, and labels each circle with a cutout and corresponding card. Using plants from her flower garden and wildflowers they gathered, children take turns identifying each plant part by placing it inside the correct circle. Each child is able to complete the task and learn about plants.

Using natural objects (plants) and teacher-made ones (cutouts), children could see, feel, and manipulate, rather than just talk about plants. This approach made the lesson understandable to *all* the children, not just to those who were fluent in English. This teacher also had children answer not just orally but also physically, by picking up and placing the plant parts in the yarn circles. This helps children who learn better using their sense of touch/movement.

Interactive approaches are important for group work, as well. The "talking drawings" strategy, suitable for second-graders, is a good example (Paquette, Fello, & Jalongo 2007):

- First, ask children to draw their understanding of a concept or object in the subject being studied—for example, if science is the subject, they might draw bats. After their initial drawings are complete, children discuss them with a partner. Then, as the teacher reads an information book about the subject, children listen carefully for details that would improve their drawings. The teacher shares several examples of labeled drawings, such as the diagrams found in textbooks for children.

- Children then draw again, incorporating as many details as they can recall. They then compare and contrast their drawings with the drawings of their classmates.

By comparing the "before" and "after" drawings, the teacher can assess how well children listened. (For more on interactive listening activities, see Birbili 2006; Gallenstein 2005; Opitz & Zbaracki 2004.)

5. Use technology to support all listeners

There are many ways we can use technology to support young children's particular strengths and adapt to their limitations as listeners. A good place to begin is *sound amplification*, which uses any of several methods to make classroom interactions audible to as many children as possible. Think of it as being "glasses for the ears" (De-Anda 2000).

As is the case with many assistive devices, tools for sound amplification can range from high tech to low tech (Flexer 1997). For example, a rolled-up piece of paper used as a megaphone out on the playground is a low tech solution. A high tech solution is a hand-held or headset microphone and sound system. Such high-quality audio technology can overcome poor classroom acoustics, allow the teacher's voice to be heard over background noise, and distribute excellent sound quality throughout the room, so that it is not too loud up front or too soft in the back ("Addressing audio needs of every learner" 2004).

Sound amplification would be worth the investment if it could help just a few children to learn—but it can do much more than that. The evidence is that sound amplification can help many children, particularly those at greatest risk of academic difficulty, by increasing student participation, attentiveness, and performance. Experts give it high marks for helping English language learners and for supporting literacy learning by enhancing listening comprehension (Crandell 1996; DeAnda 2000).

Skouge, Rao, and Boisvert (2007) suggest many other ways to use various types of technology in the classroom for children with and without hearing impairments:

For most children. Use professionally recorded, unabridged *audiobooks* (both fiction and nonfiction) in CD, tape, or online format. Audiobooks support listening comprehension, give children independent access to literature, encourage multiple readings, and allow children to make good use of time they spend riding in a car, for example (Grover & Hannegan 2005). Because most young children can understand what they hear much sooner than what they can read in print, audiobooks let children work with material that is above their actual reading level. If the goal is to support children's print reading, choose audiobooks that allow the child to control the pace of narration, so he can follow along in the companion written text (Bergman 2005).

Create a *listening library* of book and tape/CD combinations sealed in plastic bags that children can check out during the day or take home. Provide both commercially recorded and homemade sets; if you create your own, be certain your recordings include an audible signal, such as a click, to indicate to the child when it is time to turn the page. Set up a classroom *listening center* where children can gather to listen together. Provide a cassette/CD player, recordings to listen to, an audio splitter, and several sets of headphones.

Electronic tools include software that can coach students to properly pronounce each phoneme in a word by using graphics and slow-motion video to demonstrate the sound and its corresponding mouth and tongue positions. For older children, you might provide *speaking spell-check* and *speaking word processor software* to help them correct their own mistakes. The programs let them hear back what they write.

For children who are deaf or have hearing impairments. Use prerecorded *videos that include an American Sign Language interpretation* of key words in a story. Or ask college students specializing in working with children who are deaf to produce some for the class. Use a digital video camera to create your own recordings of picture books, poems, songs, presentations by guest speakers, or field trips that included an ASL interpreter.

A low tech idea would be to provide *ASL flashcards,* so children who are deaf can teach hearing children some basic signs.

For English language learners. Create *stories on tape in the child's home language.* For example, use wordless books to prompt a child's original storytelling, record it, type an accompanying text, and send both home with the child to share with his family. Or invite families to tell a children's story from their culture and record it in their home language. Use *bilingual audiobooks* so that children can follow along in the printed texts, thereby building fluency and expanding vocabulary.

For children with attentional problems. *Give the child a task.* For example, make an audio recording of a Big Book that signals when to turn the page; put the child in charge of turning the pages, using a pointer, or leading a book discussion.

Build and sustain interest by using the extra features available with some audiobooks, such as music, sound effects, or interviews with the authors (Mediatore 2003). Or use a digital camera to photograph a significant event in the child's classroom life. Have the child dictate a story to accompany the series of photographs, record it, and put the story in the listening center for all to enjoy and the child to revisit.

To *calm and focus the child* during an activity, play relaxing music softly in the background; this can enhance learning (Crncec, Wilson, & Prior 2006). Or use a soft, furry, and calm classroom pet, such as a guinea pig; studies show that stroking the fur of a mellow animal can reduce the physiological signs of stress (Jalongo 2003).

For children who are blind. There are several ways you can help children to experience literature by listening (Holum & Gahala 2001). Make *audio recordings of picture books;* read the story expressively and narrate the pictures, as well. Create *original books in Braille* using a hand embosser; assemble the pages into a three-ring binder. You also can use *commercial audiobooks.*

For children new to the class. Use a video camera to create a *silent video tour* of the classroom and the children in it. Then narrate an overview of class routines, recording versions on computer in English, Spanish, and any other languages spoken by the children. Burn them onto DVDs so children can share them with their families. Or make a greeting video in which each child says his or her name while holding up a card with his or her first name printed on it, to help newcomers learn their classmates' names.

Conclusion

As described in this chapter, the obstacles to effective listening are numerous, including hearing impairments of varying degrees, lack of appropriate models for listening and learning, learning disabilities, attention deficits, behavior disorders, specific language impairments in the area of comprehension, and difficulty in adapting to the classroom's academic language (Swain, Harrington, & Friehe 2004). Basically this means that *all* teachers must continually support children as listeners in every way they can—always beginning "where children are." Evelyn was one of my particular challenges in this regard:

> Evelyn was an 8-year-old who, according to the school psychologist's report, was the product of incest between a father and his 14-year-old daughter. Her entire family was ostracized in the community; and Evelyn was rejected even within her own family. She was frail, small for her age, and her mental capability was comparable to a 4-year-old's. She had failed kindergarten once and first grade once already when she became one of my first-graders.
>
> I noticed that the one subject Evelyn enjoyed was art. One day, after she had fashioned a remarkably detailed tree branch, bird's nest, and eggs out of clay, I promised her, "Tomorrow I'll put your name on it and put it in the display case across from the office." "What's *tomorrow*?" Evelyn asked. "Wednesday," I said—then I realized that wasn't what she meant. "Oh! *Tomorrow* is the day after today. It will be in there after you go home and come back to school on the bus." With time I got better at interpreting Evelyn's spare language, and we learned how to communicate. But at the end of the year she still could not read, and I felt I had failed her.

A journal article prompted me to think again about what Evelyn may have gained in my class. It was a study of community perspectives on school quality in which the authors concluded, "Teachers may think that their legacy is the subject content they will teach their students…what mattered [to community members] were the hidden curriculum issues, the off-the-cuff comments, words of advice, and acts of kindness and compassion exhibited by their teachers" (Bushman & Buster 2002, 32). With this in mind, I thought back to my year with Evelyn. I wished she had learned to read; but thinking back, perhaps I had succeeded in meeting her needs in other ways:

> It had been my custom to send a letter during the summer to each child coming into my classroom that fall. When Evelyn arrived on the first day of school, she had had the tattered letter in her hand—she told me it was the only piece of mail she had ever received. The rest of the time Evelyn spent in our elementary school, she never failed to give me a hug when she saw me and would stop by after school to chat.

As teachers we have only limited power to make academic goals important to a child in such desperate circumstances, like Evelyn.

What we can do under difficult conditions, however, is make our classrooms a safe haven, do our best to see to it that children's basic needs are met, and—perhaps most important of all—be thoughtful, compassionate listeners.

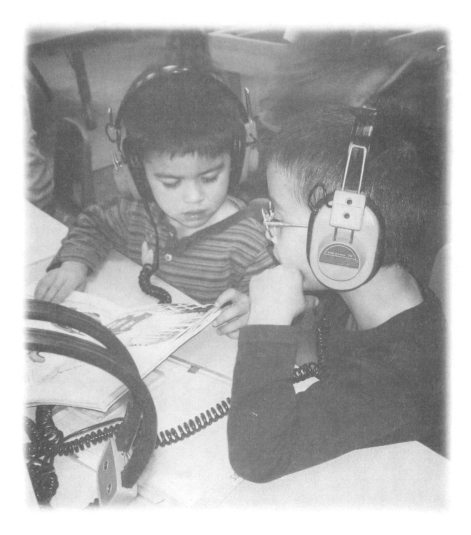

Chapter 4

Strategies to Promote Listening Skills

Improved listening skills will not necessarily result in improved listening. [Listeners] must apply these skills. We must be convinced that it pays to listen.

—Donald L. Kirkpatrick

Studies show that multisensory, multimedia methods, such as the one the teacher uses in the story below, improve listening comprehension, particularly if the children have communication difficulties (Seo 2002):

> In preparation for a field trip to the zoo, a New Orleans teacher decides to share a song that represents the musical traditions of their region— "They All Asked for You," by Buckwheat Zydeco. Before the children listen to the song, she talks with them about how people ask after or inquire about someone: That they might say, for example, "Where's your little brother today?" or, "How's your mom doing?" The children offer examples from their experience, such as "Are you coming to the picnic?" and "Is she your cousin?" and "Is your grandpa out of the hospital yet?" Then the teacher asks them to imagine, if the animals could talk, how they might inquire about the children who visit them. Then she introduces the song.

Here are the beginning lyrics of the song:

> "When I went on down to the Audubon Zoo, they all asked for you.
> They all asked for you, they even inquired about you.
> When I went on down to the Audubon Zoo, they all asked for you.
> The monkey asked. The lion asked. The elephant asked me, too."

The song continues with more and more animals inquiring "about you":

> After listening to the song once, the teacher gives each child a picture book she has made by typing the song lyrics, combining them with animal clip art, and stapling the pages together. With additional practice, the children memorize the song and sing it with enthusiasm on the trip back and forth to the zoo. Cassie, a child with Down syndrome, uses her copy of the book to name all of the animals; while Tyler, who has not had much experience with books, uses his familiarity with the song to pretend to read, gaining confidence as an emergent reader. Marisol is gifted with language; she has learned to "finger-point read" (Uhry 2002) already, so she matches the words she hears in the song with the words she sees on the page.

Each child in the class enjoys and learns from the experience because their teacher made sure it offered multiple modes of participating. Most learners in general, and young children specifically, prefer to have some visual component in a lesson (Gilbert 2005), such as this teacher's picture book of the song.

Research helps explain why interactive and multisensory listening activities are appropriate and effective:

- The most powerful influences on a learner's behavior are concrete, vivid images (Jensen 1998; 2006).

- Neuroimaging technology shows which areas of the brain are activated during various activities. It indicates that complex cognitive processes such as reading, writing, listening to and playing music, and creating art stimulate activity in *multiple areas* throughout the brain (Jensen 2006). Such multisensory activities also support effective, active listening.

- Outside of school, children often rely on visual images, physical activity, and symbolic representation—rather than on the printed word—to communicate (Rushton & Larkin 2001). Incorporation of these elements helps to bridge the difference between the experiences that children bring from home to school and the experiences that children have in school itself.

- Activities that allow for social and emotional responses and are less wedded to a strictly defined subject area reach many types of learners; "pure drill" on academic skills in narrowly defined subject areas reaches fewer types. When children are *actively en-*

gaged in learning they perform better on literacy measures than do children who are expected to keep quiet and still (Hyson, Hirsh-Pasek, & Rescorla 1990). When teachers use multisensory approaches, they are giving diverse groups of students the best chance to succeed in literacy.

- *Repetition* of a thought, idea, or experience appears to thicken the myelin sheath of the brain's cells. It is believed that thicker myelin results in faster recall and improved memory (Diamond & Hopson 1998; Rushton & Larkin 2001). Stories and songs for young children often repeat words and phrases and therefore enhance children's memory.

Challenges to developing good listening skills

Despite the obvious importance of listening in focusing children's attention and supporting their learning, early childhood settings typically contain numerous obstacles to children's listening effectively, as well as to their developing good listening habits and skills. This section looks at three categories of obstacles: within the physical environment (*context*), within the child (*learner*), and within the *teacher*.

Context variables

Classrooms can be particularly challenging—that is, *poor*—listening environments. There could be multiple reasons for this:

- Poor acoustics and reverberation can distort messages (Petry, McClellan, & Myler 2001).
- Physical distance from the speaker can vary greatly for each child and during different activities, making the speaker difficult to hear.
- Background noise inside the classroom (e.g., from heating or air conditioning units or vents, audio/visual equipment, moving chairs, children's voices); outside the classroom (children in the hallway, sounds from other classrooms); and outside the building (traffic, lawnmowers, children on the playground) all compete with the message (ASHA 2004).
- Frequent interruptions (e.g., visitors, the loudspeaker) can break children's focus.

Learner variables

"Listen to me"—how often adults say that to young children. If only getting children to be good listeners were that simple. In fact, what we expect of children when we ask them to listen may be more complex than we realize:

> Receptive language ability requires attending to the speech of another person and interpreting the grammatical constructions used to construct the message, as well as the meaning of the words in the context of the discourse situation and the linguistic structure. In addition, interpreting the message involves sufficient short-term memory and attention to keep track of what is said, and to integrate it into the context of earlier speech and situations, as well as to relate it to any background knowledge that the speaker is assuming as shared and relevant. These are very demanding skills that require considerable practice. (Nelson 2007, 167)

To be good listeners (i.e., to listen effectively or actively), young children need capacity, willingness, and constructive habits. *Capacity* refers to whether or not the child is capable (physically, cognitively, emotionally) of hearing and making sense of the message. As discussed in Chapter 3, hearing loss or impairment, attentional disorders, emotional disturbances, illness, language proficiency, distractions such as hunger, and so on, can all interfere with a child's capacity to listen.

Willingness has to do with motivation: Does the child recognize a need to listen? For example, does she understand that if she listens to instructions on how to use the new software, then it can become a useful tool? That if he listens to his peers respond to his story as he sits in the author's chair, his story can be appreciated and he may get suggestions for improving it? Having a good reason to listen increases a child's willingness, and effective teachers are careful to point out the tangible, immediate benefits of careful listening.

Habits refers to a child's characteristic behavioral responses to listening situations; for example, a toddler might prepare for a bedtime story at home by getting into pajamas, holding a favorite stuffed toy, and getting settled under the covers. A second-grader reading independently at home might curl up with the family cat in a beanbag chair. At school, when teachers do things such as sing songs to signal the end of center time, they not only create routines that smooth transitions but also teach children good listening habits.

As the children's comments in the box on the next page reflect, children typically have a basic understanding that capacity, willingness, and habits play roles in good listening—even if they are not always successful in acting on that understanding. Notice that many of the children's ideas about listening focus on being obedient, keeping out of trouble, acting passively, or earning a reward. But effective listening bears only a slight resemblance to that. True, listening is a way to take in information and to please adults. But it is also, for example, a basis for establishing relationships, planning a course of action, and finding enjoyment in listening to music or stories. In *active listening* particularly, the listener not only gets the message right but also becomes an involved participant by asking questions or acting on what was heard.

Children, however, may not yet have what it takes to be active listeners. In a 1990 study of children's ideas about listening, Teresa McDevitt found that even when young children were deliberately given an ambiguous message, they assumed that their inability to understand was *their* fault, rather than realizing that the message itself was confusing. Young children may not feel sufficiently confident or assertive to ask for clarification when they do not understand (McDevitt & Ormrod 2007).

McDevitt (1990) also concluded that the status differential between young children and adults often causes children to feel it is not their place to ask for clarification. It is also important to note that in some cultures, it is considered disrespectful for children to ask adults questions.

Teacher variables

Chapter 1 suggests that, rather than assuming that children's listening problems are inside them, we teachers sometimes need to look inside ourselves. That was something the teacher in the following story should have done:

> "Early in September I received a call from a colleague at my university who wanted to talk to someone in the Early Childhood Education Department. She had a concern about her son, a 6-year-old who didn't want to go to school. The reason, the child said, was 'Because my teacher yells at us all of the time.' The mother had witnessed the teacher yelling on more than one occasion, but she and her husband

Children's Ideas about Listening at School

In interviews conducted by Jennifer Drumm, Emily Kent, and Katie Klann, all graduate students from Edinboro University of Pennsylvania, children ages 5–8 were asked questions about their listening skills:

What does it mean to listen?

"Not to screw it up. Listen to directions."

"People use ears to listen to other people. If you don't listen, you can't hear what the teacher is saying."

"You get to hear stories."

"It is when you pay attention."

"Listen to the teacher so you get smarter, grow up, and go to college."

"To hear what somebody says."

How can you tell if someone is listening?

"When they're being quiet. When they are trying to think…like a guessing game, thinking inside."

"You see it in the face—quiet."

"Because they look at me and talk to me."

"Their eyes need to be on the speaker."

"If they are looking at their shoe or talking to someone else, then they are not listening. They are in la-la land!"

"They talk when I am done."

"If they answer you."

Are you a good listener? How do you know?

"Yes, I am quiet."

"Yes, because I am from China."

"Yeah—I usually get my work done right."

"Yes, because my teachers say 'good listening.'"

"Yes. I look at the teacher, follow directions, and wait to tie my shoe if it needs to be tied."

"Yes, I look at people when they are talking to me."

"Yes, I don't talk when the teacher talks."

How can listening help you?

"Because it helps you not ask questions that people have already said."

"If you want to get smarter or drive, then you need to listen."

"You will get in trouble if you do not listen."

"Listening helps me learn in school."

"So you know the rules and you won't get sent to the principal's office."

"If you listen you can get a reward."

"If someone tells you something important, you know it."

Learning to Listen, Listening to Learn

had been trying to reassure themselves that they were being over-protective. Maybe her son just needed time to adjust. Then one night, she overheard him end his bedtime prayers with '…and if I should die before I wake, please make it be on Sunday night so that I don't have to go to school.' When she asked for my advice, I told her if it were my son, I would get him out of that class as quickly as possible.

"Coincidentally, the following week I was scheduled to supervise student teachers at that very school for the first time. When I got there, I saw (and heard) for myself this first grade teacher, loudly berating her class for 'not listening.' Passing teachers ducked their heads and hurried by; the principal, one of my former students, went into his office and closed the door."

This terrible teacher was a source of anxiety for children, anguish for parents, and mortification for colleagues. The intent of the story is not to make teachers look bad; fortunately, such behavior is atypical. Rather, the purpose is to show how a teacher is always a major variable in whether children do—or don't—develop good listening skills. We should expect that teachers very rarely are the problem. But they are always part of the solution to a child's listening challenges through the teaching choices they make regarding *pedagogy, curriculum,* and *assessment.*

Planning pedagogy that supports children's listening

Here are some typical pedagogical problems or challenges, each followed by some possible solutions that support children's listening:

Long, complicated messages, such as a set of directions, demand a lot of children's working memory, making the message difficult for young children to hold in their minds and act on; therefore…

- Break up directions into short, sequential steps; reinforce spoken messages with pictures, audio recordings, and printed prompts and reminders.

- Pause between each step to allow children time to process its information.

- Model procedures yourself; guide children in physically rehearsing them.

- Ask children to recap/review the steps in a procedure, rather than you doing it. This also lets children to do more of the talking.

Messages that are unclear or that children don't perceive as directed at them often are ignored or forgotten; therefore…

- State *why* a message is important, and *for whom* it is important.

- Strive for complete clarity in your messages.

- Ask children questions about a message; this encourages them to reflect on the content and monitor their comprehension (Reid 1991; White 2002).

- Always check for understanding before letting children begin independent or group work.

- Use media tie-ins to tap into children's prior knowledge. For example, a child with limited book experience might be very familiar with television and movie depictions of the ideas found in books (Kenedeou et al. 2005).

Young children are easily distracted, so they need help focusing and listening; therefore…

- Come up with an engaging method for getting children's attention. For example, introduce a shy puppet who will not venture out into the classroom until the children are quiet.

- Together with the children, list sources of distracting background noises as they occur, then discuss ways to counteract them.

- Make sure that both the physical arrangement of the classroom and its procedures support listening (e.g., clearly define a space designated a "quiet area," establish that a pleasant sound such as wind chimes will always announce story time).

- Have children respond more actively (e.g., "When you hear a pair of rhyming words, put your hands on your shoulders").

- Establish listening cues. For example, as an everyday attention-getter, teach children that when you say, "Attention Button" to look at you and pretend to press an imaginary button on the top of their heads. Teach children a different signal to instantly stop what they are doing and await instructions, such as "Freeze!"; use this only for emergencies.

Learning to Listen, Listening to Learn

- Invest in some text-to-speech or speech-to-text software and teach children how to use it (Cassell 2004). Hearing print transformed into talk or watching as words are converted to print provides a more multisensory experience related to listening.

Children need an ever expanding vocabulary to be effective listeners; therefore…

- Capitalize on each child's interests and follow his or her "agenda" in conversation (White 2002).

- Ask for more elaborated responses, rather than one-word answers; children do not operate at their highest level of communication when their answers are abbreviated.

- Balance asking questions that have one right answer with asking more open-ended questions that have many possible responses (Dyson 1987).

- Provide a variety of opportunities for extended conversation among peers (Fraser & Skolnick 1994), such as a nonfiction book club in which children listen to a book and then discuss it together (Heller 2007).

- Provide a diversity of listening experiences that introduce new words in new contexts (e.g., recorded songs, audiobooks, storytelling web sites, a walk to identify nature sounds).

Children with poor listening habits often need direct coaching to replace them with effective ones; therefore…

- Model giving undivided attention, and schedule time for you to give it to each child (e.g., a one-to-one lunch, a talk on the playground).

- Demonstrate to children that we listen with our ears but that other parts of the body (e.g., eyes, feet, mouth, hands) can be the "helpers" (Merkel-Piccini 2001). Looking (e.g., viewing the pictures as a story is read), using feet and hands (e.g., participating in an action song), and using speech (e.g., joining in a refrain on cue) help children to get involved and pay attention.

- Teach children what to listen for during a story; use props, such as cue cards that indicate *who* (with a silhouette of the character);

what (stick people performing various actions); *when* (clock); *where* (map); and *why* (question mark).

- Give children practice *restating* ("Who can tell me the first thing you need to do if you want to play a CD?"); *summarizing* ("What did we do on our trip to the post office?"); *reflecting* ("If you could have any animal for a pet, what would you choose and why?"); and *self-assessing* ("Which story do you think is your best?").

Integrating listening throughout the curriculum

Listening truly is interdisciplinary, so it should be emphasized and incorporated throughout the day and across subject areas. Some suggestions for accomplishing this follow (Jalongo 1991):

Participating in discussions. Instead of the traditional Show and Tell, consider an alternative that requires more listening from the child who is presenting, called "Show and Ask." Invite each child to bring an interesting object to school (no expensive toys) and, rather than having the child to make an oral presentation (as in Show and Tell), have the other children ask questions about the object.

The audience in "Show and Ask" has greater responsibility for participating and asking good questions to support listening skills, not only for the speaker but also for the audience. When 4-year-old Becky shared a knit scarf with the class, some of the questions from her classmates were: "Did somebody make it?" ("Yes, my Grandma knitted it"); "Did you get to pick the color?" ("It was a surprise, but pink is my favorite anyway"); and "How did she do the fringey part?" ("I didn't see, but I can ask her. I know she puts knots in there, see?").

When we teach children how to ask questions and participate in discussions, it is particularly important for them to understand that the speaker usually *does* know the answer and that a good questioner usually *does not* ask a question to which he already knows the answer. For example, if Santos is sharing a collection of plastic animals, a good questioner might ask, "Where did you get them?" or, "Can I play with them later?" Conversely, it is not a good question to ask,

"How many are there?" after the child has lined up two tigers and three lions on the carpet, because the answer to this question is apparent.

The box beginning on the next page describes a similar way to build children's questioning skills with "sharing centers." (For more tips on designing activities and leading discussions, see Kirkland & Patterson 2005; Kratcoski & Katz 1998; Nespeca 2005.)

Reflective listening. Discuss listening during group time with questions such as "How does it feel to have someone listen to you?" You model reflective listening when you ask a child to share her thoughts on a topic, then, as the child speaks, sit quietly and look at her; once the child finishes, restate what she said. Conclude with, "Does anyone remember something else that Kate said?"

Move to the next child and say, "Let's see how well we listen. Listen carefully to Manuel and when he's finished, raise your hand if you can tell me something that he said." Invite children to share what they remember. Check back with the speaker to see whether the children's recollections are correct. This validates both the speaker and the listeners (Church 2006).

Sing a song to the tune of "Are You Sleeping?" with these lyrics:

> Are you listening, are you listening?
> To our friend, to our friend.
> What did Lisa tell us, what did Lisa tell us?
> Share it please, share it please. (Church 2006)

"Say something about..." To tie in with a curricular theme, assemble a small group of children and have each contribute a statement about that theme. For example, you might prompt, "Say something about...families," "...celebrations," "...the ocean." Children's comments reveal what content they have learned as well as their particular insight into the topic.

Classroom museum. Older children can contribute a photograph of a treasured family item to a formal display of four or five other photographs. Record each child telling the family story surrounding the object in the same sequence as the display; make sure to use an audible signal (e.g., a bell) to prompt the listener to move to the next item. Children listen to the stories as they view the photographs, just like an audio tour at a museum. After everyone has listened to a set of stories and the display has been up a while, do the

continued on p. 82

Sharing Centers: An Alternative to "Show and Tell"
by Kathleen Dailey

Sharing centers offer a child-centered alternative to Show and Tell that encourages young children to use language in meaningful contexts. Based on the concept of learning centers, in sharing centers children work in small, interactive groups of four to five, organized around their needs and interests. These small group interactions promote development of receptive and expressive language, self-esteem, the concept of *audience*, cognitive skills, and social skills. Unlike Show and Tell, the sharing centers approach gives children many opportunities to ask questions, explore items, and learn from one another. They learn to listen attentively and to respond thoughtfully through meaningful dialogue, as in this example:

> **Jason** (Displays a picture album): "This is my dog, Jake."
> **Emily:** "He looks like my dog."
> **Kevin:** "My dog is a little bigger than that."
> **Shawn:** "Look how he sticks his tongue out. The water's dripping on the floor."
> **Kevin:** "Do you give him a bath? In the bathtub?"
> **Jason:** "Yeah, he likes it and he shakes the soap all over."

During the exchange, the children remained actively engaged throughout and they focused their interactions by talking about the items, drawing upon their experiences, asking questions, and taking turns. In the sharing center approach, the teacher acts as a facilitator rather than as a director. She guides the children in their learning and language development and serves as a participant, learner, and observer of children's social, cognitive, and language skills.

A teacher considering doing sharing centers will need to (1) explain to families how it works, (2) model it for children, and (3) explain the procedure step by step. Families will want to know how sharing centers develop their children's listening skills and what kinds of items are appropriate to share. That list might include things found in nature, exotic or little-known food items, safe tools, photographs, items used in a hobby or favorite sport, children's books, scientific instruments, items from a personal collection, and so on.

The next step is for the teacher to model what it means to "share." Students gather at the carpet, and she shows them a large decorated box with "Sharing Centers" written on the side. In the box, the teacher has collected some items to share:

Teacher (Taking out a bird's nest): "A bird built this nest in a hanging basket of flowers on my front porch. The bird laid three white and gray speckled eggs in the nest. What else would you like to know about the bird or the nest? Think about what questions you could ask me about the bird or the eggs or the nest."

Nita: "What color was the bird?"

Teacher: "It was brown and white."

Chris: "Did you get to see the babies?"

Teacher: "No, the eggs never hatched."

Kyle: "I saw a nest like that in my tree."

Then the teacher describes how sharing centers will work: A chart will designate four or five children as the sharers for each day. On their day, those children each will bring in something to share, which they will put into the Sharing Centers box when they arrive. When it's time for the activity, the sharers retrieve their objects and go sit in designated "centers," located around the classroom. The remaining children are distributed among the sharing centers in heterogeneous groups. Sharing begins; every five minutes or so, depending on the interest of the group, the listeners change centers.

The teacher and children also decide on some rules for the activity, which the teacher writes out and posts. For example:

Our Rules for Sharing Centers
(1) The sharer speaks first
(2) We take turns touching the sharing object
(3) Everyone gets a chance to talk and ask questions
(4) No interrupting; no grabbing

During the activity, the teacher can walk among the groups to observe children's interactions, or enter a sharing center as a participant and role model. The teacher can encourage language development and dialogue by asking open-ended questions, such as "What else could you ask Katherine about her glasses?" "Cara and Tom, tell us, how does the bark feel to you?" "Could anyone else tell us about a time when they went fishing?" "Where could you hang your bird feeder?" "What was the best part of going to Niagara Falls with your family?"

Typically, dialogues become richer as the activity continues, as the sharer draws on prior experiences with previous audiences. As children learn the routine, they rotate easily among the centers and begin dialogues without prompting.

Kathleen Dailey is a faculty member at Edinboro University in Pennsylvania.

same with the next group of four or five children, until everyone has had the opportunity to listen to everyone's stories.

Simple surveys. Compose a simple paper survey (one or more questions, all the children's names in a list with space for their answers), asking about such things as favorite colors, favorite foods, and so forth. Give each child a copy on a clipboard and have them poll their classmates. Having to refer to and record answers on the sheet by each child's name and to approach each child individually, children build social skills and practice recognizing names. Compile the data into a simple bar graph by printing each child's name on a self-adhesive note, then arranging the notes to represent the children's responses.

Invented stories. As children progress through the primary grades, they become more capable of thinking from a point of view different from their own; for example, from a toy's. Read aloud several books that tell a story from a toy's point of view, then have children invent a story about the life of a toy, draw a picture of that toy, and record the toy's story so that others can listen to it. Listening to stories, inventing new ones, and retelling them all work to support children's listening skills, and encourage children to associate listening with enjoyment (Bishop & Kimball 2006). Explore other activities that build on stories, like discussing alternative beginnings or endings, comparing and contrasting characters, creating sound effects or a musical accompaniment, and taking turns to retell the story.

Interviews. Interviewing is a good way to develop children's listening skills. Rather than inviting a guest to make a presentation with only a little time for questions at the end, let the children work together in advance to prepare interesting interview questions. This preparation gets children more involved during the presentation, as they ask questions and listen for the answers. It also helps speakers to adjust their presentation to a particular audience of children.

Experiments. When a group of children discovered ants in their sandbox, they shared what they knew about ants with each other—but some of their information was contradictory. One child's grandmother had told her that ants like sugar; another said that they like grease. The teacher suggested an experiment. Children placed a cube of sugar at one end of the sandbox and a piece of bologna at the other, then watched to see which food the ants preferred. Children took turns drawing the ants' behavior, listened to information books about the different types of ants, and listened to one another as observations of the ants were shared.

Listening games. "Simon Says" and the like have been part of early childhood curriculum for decades. For a new listening game, pick a category—for example, favorite foods. The first child begins: "I am Tyler and I like tacos." The next child follows: "I am Ming and I like spaghetti, and Tyler likes tacos." The next child: "I am Celeste and I like pizza. Ming likes spaghetti, and Tyler likes tacos." Before playing this small group game, reassure children that everyone will help them remember if they get stuck. (For more listening games, see Torbert 2005.)

"How does that work?" During a session on cooking, a teacher noticed that children were fascinated by her common kitchen gadgets (garlic press, spiral potato cutter, and orange juicer, to name just a few). So she told the class, "Choose the object you find most interesting. Explore it yourselves, then I will explain and show you how to use it while you listen. Then you will explain how it works to someone else."

Describe and draw. Children work with a partner; one is the speaker, the other the listener. The speaker describes something very familiar to him—like a favorite t-shirt—and the listener draws the item based on what the speaker says. After the speaker sees the drawing, he can give additional information so the listener can revise her drawing accordingly.

Storylines. After listening to a story, children can check their listening comprehension by arranging the story's events in the correct sequence. Another option would be drawing a map of a character's travels.

Ten-minute recordings. Provide an inexpensive, durable audio-cassette recorder, plug-in microphone, and blank 10-minute tapes so children can record their own listening material. For young children, add a green sticker on the Play button and a red sticker on the Stop button as reminders. The box on p. 84 suggests some appropriate listening activities.

Ten Listening Activities with 10-Minute Tapes

1) Record a simple, no-bake recipe for a snack that children can draw and eat. Children who are drawing representationally can also draw a rebus recipe, as a check on their listening comprehension.

2) Whenever a guest visits the classroom and reads a book aloud, record it. Put the tape and book together in a resealable plastic bag, and add it to the listening library.

3) Collect folk tales and nursery rhymes from all the cultures represented in the class. Ask families to record them in their culture's own language and in English, for a bilingual listening library.

4) Record basic words (*yes, no, please, thank you*, numbers, days of the week) in each of the languages spoken by children in the class. By listening to these simple words, children build on their understanding of different cultures and learn about their classmates.

5) Have one child interview another; the question should be open-ended, to prompt an elaborated answer, such as "What do you like about school?"

6) Record children as they tell a story, sing a song, or read aloud to begin collecting an audio portfolio of their work. Recordings made across the year will become a record of the child's language growth. Periodically send a recording home so the family can listen to the child's progress.

7) Have children record audio "greeting cards" for their family members or for classmates who have moved away, are traveling, or are ill.

8) At an open house or after a musical performance, ask families and other guests to record positive messages for the children.

9) Get children who are reading independently to record poetry together. Books such as *Farmer's Garden: Rhymes for Two Voices* (Harrison), *Joyful Noise: Poems for Two Voices* (Fleischman), and *Wham! It's a Poetry Jam: Discovering Performance Poetry* (Holbrook) explain how to do this activity.

10) Ask a musician to record the melodies of several of the children's favorite songs so they can sing along; record their singing.

Source: Based on Buckleitner (2000).

Teaching children to listen to one another

A first grade teacher confided,

> "My biggest problem with listening is when children have to listen to one another. I usually can get them to pay attention to me, but when a classmate speaks very quietly or has trouble expressing ideas, the children's attention wanes. I have pretty much given up on group discussions in kindergarten because it seems like I have to jump in or I have a bunch of wiggling, distracted children."

As a first step, consider whether you truly value children's contributions in your classroom—or whether yours is the only authoritative voice. If children's main reason for speaking is to be validated by you, they have no clear reason to listen to one another. Their role is merely to wait for you to determine the legitimacy of their answers. Conversely, in classrooms where children's contributions are truly valued, they have good reasons to listen to one another. They listen and speak to be understood and appreciated, to persuade each other, or to revise their ideas based on new information (Aukerman 2006).

Once you have reflected on what your classroom practice says about the value you place on what children say, here are some practical suggestions for supporting children in listening to one another:

- **Demonstrate how a listener shows respect for a speaker.** Look at the speaker, be quiet when the speaker is speaking, and ask good questions. Let children do more of the talking so that they will be doing more of the thinking.

- **Model careful listening while a child is speaking.** Resist the urge to use that time to do other teaching tasks; otherwise, you are sending the message that the child's words are not important to you.

- **Pair children of mixed language skills.** Having a conversational partner who is a "more accomplished" speaker is a very important way to support language development.

- **Set children up for listening success.** Avoid situations where children are expected to listen for extended periods of time. Alternate opportunities to listen and speak.

- **Keep groups small.** Young children seldom function well in large groups that leave them waiting to participate. As a general rule of thumb, use the children's age as a guide—about three children in a small group for 3-year-olds, four for 4-year-olds, and so forth.

- **Teach the difference between a comment and a question.** For example, when a child was sharing a large plastic dinosaur, a *question* from a 4-year-old was, "Does its legs move?" Another classmate made the *comment*, "I have plastic dinosaurs, too, but they aren't that big." Point out the difference to children, and practice asking questions and sharing comments.

- **Coach children in how to project their voices and be heard.** Use a microphone, if available, to encourage children to speak audibly. An inexpensive home karaoke machine or other sound amplification can help. Sometimes a child who is very quiet will speak more loudly during creative drama or when taking on a different role represented by a puppet.

- **Use a prop to recognize the speaker.** One class used a squishy, heart-shaped pillow to show who had the floor. Help children to understand that only the person with that object is permitted to talk.

- **Practice discussion skills.** Encourage children to express their ideas, guide them in determining whether ideas are repeats, urge them to stay on task, and model careful listening and effective verbal expression.

- **Instead of expecting children to share solo all of the time, consider using "think, pair, and share."** Give children time to think of ideas, then pair with a partner and share with their partner or with a larger group. This can be particularly helpful for children who are reticent about speaking to the entire group.

- **Invite children to dramatize their own stories with their peers.** Set up a corner of the room as a stage and ask children to form small groups and act out something that happened to them over the weekend or create a story from their imaginations. (For more on how story dramatizations and listening can support speaking and writing, see Paley 2004 and her NAEYC videos; Horn 2005.)

- **Have children construct and use props and visual aids that support their talk.** Props might include photographs, flannel board cutouts, posters, masks, and simple costumes.

- **Give children meaningful occasions to speak and listen.** For example, "Plan, Do, Review" is part of the High/Scope curriculum. Children meet in small groups to decide which centers and activities they will pursue (plan), complete the activities (do), and then meet again afterwards to report on what they have accomplished (review). Such conversations encourage children to listen to one another.

- **Videotape sharing sessions, then debrief with individual children.** Help them see what they can do to communicate more effectively, both as speakers and as listeners.

Making conversational space in our classrooms for children to speak and listen to one another takes some effort. But many teachers notice the benefits, as this second grade teacher did: "I am learning to let children do more of the talking, and I am doing more listening. As I pull out, they seem to listen better to each other—I wonder if they learn more from peers than from teachers?" (Fraser & Skolnick 1994, 146).

Assessing children's listening

Just about every test we give young children is in some sense a test of listening: Children have to listen to verbal instructions to perform the task, or if a test is individually administered, the child often must respond to questions that are presented verbally.

There are three basic ways to assess children's listening specifically: (1) hearing screenings and tests, (2) standardized tests that evaluate listening comprehension, and (3) observations of children's listening behavior. Tests of children's hearing are an essential first step when listening difficulties are suspected or have surfaced; these were covered in Chapter 3. This next section focuses on the remaining two methods.

Standardized tests

In a survey of Michigan teachers attending a summer workshop, "listening" was identified as the topic they most wanted to discuss. A listening comprehension section had just been added to their state-mandated assessments, and their students had performed poorly on it.

In addition to states' own assessments, there are also commercial standardized tests that assess different aspects of listening. The most common may be the Peabody Picture Vocabulary Test (PPVT-IV), which assesses receptive oral language by having the child select the correct picture from four choices to match the word spoken by the examiner. Another test commonly used with young children, the Dynamic Indicators of Basic Early Literacy Skills (DIBELS), includes a section on listening comprehension. For older children, the individually administered Oral and Written Language Scales (OWLS) evaluates written and oral language, including listening comprehension. (For more on screenings and formal assessment methods, see Miller 2007.)

Observation

To the degree that they are *valid* (correctly measure what they were designed to test) state assessments and other standardized tests can tell us what children have learned both by listening and about how to listen. But such tests are summative rather than formative, and they occur under artificial conditions. For teachers in the classroom, a much more important and pedagogically useful method is to assess listening by carefully observing children's behavior. That's what the teacher did in this vignette:

> In the computer lab, a kindergartner commented that the yellow dog icon that the software was using to fetch files and answer questions "looked like a Labrador retriever." His teacher asked, "Do you know what it means to *retrieve*?" to which he replied, "It means you go and get something, and then you bring it back."

She hadn't directly observed this boy when he learned what *retrieve* meant; but because he was not yet reading, she could assume that he had heard the word used in context and had taken its meaning as his own. Since we cannot directly observe listening itself, because it is mostly internal (Adelmann 2005), we must surmise from answers such as this boy's whether children are listening effectively.

Whether we observe children in a naturalistic setting (e.g., by listening in on their small group discussions or during dramatic play) or during a more structured activity, observing a child's listening puts us in the position of making inferences based on behavior (Smith 2001). A multifaceted approach to listening assessment that combines different types of assessment (e.g., hearing tests, language test results, teacher observations, input from the family) supplies a well-rounded picture of each child's listening capabilities. For example, observations in a large group setting offer another perspective, as in this example:

> A guest speaker was taking questions from the group of 64 kindergartners and did not know their names. She made eye contact with one boy and said, "Okay, you, in the red and white striped shirt." All of the adults in the room smiled when the boy glanced down at his shirt to check what he was wearing before he responded.

From his behavior, we can infer that he had been listening.

We know that children do not operate at their highest level of communication when "quizzed" or closely monitored by teachers (Dyson 1987). So their listening behavior during play and in informal conversations are particularly valuable pieces of assessment information. Dramatic play requires symbolism, interactive dialogue, negotiation, role taking, acting out others' thoughts and actions, and improvisation—all of which demonstrate children's listening comprehension (Bergen 2001).

Conclusion

During recess, 7-year-old Todd wanted to organize a game that he had learned in physical education class. He called out to his classmates on the playground, but they just kept on playing. "Can you blow your whistle?" he asked the teacher. A loud tweet attracted a bit more attention, but most of the children just looked up briefly and resumed what they had been doing. "They just won't listen to me!" Todd said in exasperation. "Now you know how teachers feel sometimes," the teacher joked. Eventually, she was able to gather the group, and Todd led them in a rousing game. Afterwards, the teacher told him privately, "You did such a good job that I think they will listen to you next time."

As Todd quickly realized, winning children's attention is difficult, and the attention-grabbing strategies we use may not work right away. Here, blowing a whistle didn't have much impact, although Todd expected that it would. Despite his initial inability to grab his classmates' attention, Todd made listening "pay off" for them with the fun game he led. Because the children listened to him as he explained the game, it will most likely be easier for him to win their attention the next time.

As every effective early childhood educator understands, "Students bring diverse understandings to learning, based on their prior knowledge, language skills, cognitive processing abilities, cultural perspectives, motivations, and interests" (Lapadat 2002, 278). Effective teachers adjust their instructional language accordingly. We can, for example, talk a little or a lot, repeat ideas (or not), vary the pace of our talk, use more or less complicated sentences, state the rules for participation in different activities, pose questions at various levels, choose particular examples, and on and on. Strategies that accommodate differences between children and situations are the best way to build young children's motivation, confidence, and competency as listeners.

I Like to Hear… I Would Like to Hear…

"Rock 'n' roll music in my room." (Steven, age 8)

"I hear the flowers jiggling, the clouds bumping into each other, ladybugs crawling, a beaver chomping on a tree, a frog munching on a fly, the butterflies flapping their wings, the worm 'sliming' in the dirt." (Gwynneth, age 5)

I Like to Hear… I Would Like to Hear…

"The waves crashing and the trees blowing at the beach." (Emme, age 4)

"Chairs creaking on the front porch." (Emily, age 6)

I Like to Hear… I Would Like to Hear…

"I like to hear the sound of snakes, because they're my favorite animals. I made a cobra attacking a crane." (Sydney, age 6)

I Don't Like to Hear…

"The rain. I fell down." (Abigail, age 3)

I Don't Like to Hear...

"The crab's claws snapping." (Rachel, age 6)

"A dolphin splashing in the water. The water has waves. It is lightninging and thundering." (Zachary, age 4)

The children's artwork reproduced here, including this drawing by Molly, age 7, was collected by the author with the assistance of Connie Kerr Vogt, administrator of South Hills Child Development Center, a Reggio Emilia-based program in Erie, Pennsylvania.

Chapter 5

Helping Families Support Children's Listening

The first duty of love is to listen.
—Paul Tillich

Three troops of Cub Scouts excitedly gathered in a church basement for a children's program on dog bite prevention called Play It Safe with Dogs. First, the presenters introduced their dogs and talked briefly about the tests the animals had to pass before they could participate. Then they used posters to cover 10 basic safety rules (e.g., ask the owner before petting), invited the children to role-play the rules, and showed a short video about how to interpret dog behavior. They concluded the session with a review of the main ideas, in which children were asked to supply the reasoning behind each rule. At the end, each scout got an opportunity to demonstrate what he had learned by petting the dogs safely. As the presenters packed up, one of the scout leaders said, "I must tell you that we have had some problems in the past with these boys getting restless and distracted, but we didn't have to remind them to pay attention this evening, not even once."

This story demonstrates two important ideas about listening that relate to helping families build their children's listening skills: that children don't learn only when they are in the classroom, and that some approaches are better than others in encouraging children to listen.

Home as a context for listening

It is a common misconception that children are learning only when they are in a formal, structured educational environment. So you may need to help families understand that language learning—and the development of listening skills—also occurs in everyday situations, such as these exchanges between family members:

> Three-year-old Laura is listening to a bedtime reading of *The Gingerbread Man*. After her aunt uses a crafty-sounding voice to read the fox's lines, Laura looks surprised, peers inside her aunt's mouth, and asks, "Is that still you in there, Aunt Mia?"

> Four-year-old Lynn lives in Pennsylvania and is eager for a visit from her grandmother, who lives in Arizona. When they speak on the phone, Lynn asks, "Why don't you come over?" Her grandmother replies, "Well, I live far away, but I am coming for a visit. It will be in seven sleeps—seven times that you go to sleep and wake up. Then I'll be at your house." Lynn tells her mom about this important message, and they begin to mark the days on the calendar.

> When 5-year-old Francisco's cousins come for a visit during the summer, they make a tent with him outdoors using a clothesline and blanket. Then his cousins settle into their fort with a pile of their favorite books. After a while, Francisco's 9-year-old cousin Maria notices that Francisco is no longer with them. She finds him sitting by himself in the living room, on the verge of tears. "Everyone wants to read books but I can't read yet," Francisco says. Maria speaks with the cousins, explaining that Francisco wants to join in. She suggests that they can read to or with him, they can talk with him about the pictures, or he can recite a favorite book from memory. Soon all of the children are reading, talking, and listening happily in their tent.

Experiences such as these make a huge contribution to listening and learning throughout the early childhood years.

Families affect their children's learning through heredity of traits and characteristics, but also through the type of language environment provided in the home. For example, some families are hectic and loud, others are comparatively calm and quiet; some families consider interrupting to be rude, while others regard it as the sign of a lively conversation; and in some families the language spoken in home, school, and church is the same, while in other families it is different. Parents' attitudes toward education and their aspirations for their children, the language models they provide, literacy materials they supply, and activities they encourage all make a substantial contribution to children's language development (Stone et al. 2005; Yaden & Paratore 2003). In particular, the box on pages 96–97 offers some information you can share with families, describing the steps they can take to foster good listening habits in themselves and their children.

Families may well be aware that children "listen and learn"; but some might not realize that research tells us that certain approaches are better than others at encouraging young children to listen. Going back to the Play It Safe with Dogs example, a discussion afterwards between the presenters and the scout master surfaced the strategies the presenters used to get the scouts to listen. Specifically, the dog handlers had considered their audience in designing their presentation, made the session more interactive, and used visual aids. Here are some other speaker behaviors that effective teachers use routinely to help children listen and learn:

- **Focus**—Plan something that attracts children's attention from the start

- **Variety**—Present concepts in more than one way

- **Pacing**—Adjust the pace of the session to fit the audience

- **Guided practice**—Check for understanding along the way

- **Assessment**—Evaluate the impact of the experience

Parents and other family members may not realize it, but they probably use these approaches all of the time—or if they don't, they certainly could once we suggest it.

For example, 5-year-old Byron, a very serious little boy, was apprehensive about serving as ring bearer in his aunt's wedding. "Let me think about it," was his first response, which the adults found very amusing; with some coaxing, he did agree to participate. Knowing about his reluctance, everyone involved made a special effort to allay his anxieties. Without doing it intentionally, they used several of the listening and learning strategies above:

- **They made sure to get Byron's attention**—The bride knelt down so she was on his eye level and explained, "You get to do something very important—you'll carry my ring on a little pillow to the front of the church when Stacie tells you."

continued on p. 98

Parents, Help Support Good Listening Habits in Your Child

Understand the basics of child language development. Learn how to recognize when a child is hearing and speaking normally. The American Speech-Language-Hearing Association, for example, offers the publication *How Does Your Child Hear and Talk?* (available at www.asha.org, in English and Spanish). Another criterion often used in evaluating language development is how well a child can be understood by others. By age 3, a typically developing child can be understood about 75 percent of the time; by age 4, about 95 percent of the time (Apel & Masterson 2001).

If you have the slightest concern that your child is not hearing properly, have his hearing evaluated immediately. Technology makes it possible to evaluate hearing very early—even in infancy. The leading causes of speech problems in young children are undetected hearing impairments and ear infections that lead to fluid in the ears.

Teach your child from infancy to listen. Even though infants can't talk, they can listen and respond to many sounds—such as the tone of your voice, a lullaby, or lively music. Respond to your baby's coos, gurgles, and babblings. When you talk to her, use *child-directed speech*, in which you: (1) use exaggerated body and facial gestures to get her attention; (2) draw attention to key words by saying them louder or stretching them out (e.g., "Look at that bbbiiiigggg boat"); and (3) pause frequently throughout (e.g., "Once there were three bears...and they...").

Set an example of careful listening. Give your child your undivided attention whenever possible. Try to stop what you are doing and really listen when he talks. When adults work to improve their listening, everyone in the family benefits. Children learn as much from what we *do* as from what we say. Parents who listen have children who listen.

Make time for listening. Set up a special time for stories, books, and conversations, such as during bath time or just before bedtime. Try to discover how your child perceives her world. Set aside time every day to look at and discuss colorful, inviting books.

Expect story sharing to be different with a very young child. Families sometimes give up on sharing books with their very young child because the child doesn't sit still and quietly listen from start to finish. It's not that he won't—he *can't*, at least until he's older. To make story time more enjoyable, first ask a children's librarian to suggest some books suitable for his age group. Then modify your expectations: Realize, for example, that to a toddler, "reading" might be pointing to pictures on the page and making one-word comments. Rather than just reading along, ask him *who, what,* and *where* questions about the pictures. Make the book "all about him" so reading becomes a conversation: "Look, he's playing with a ball. Do you have a ball?"… "Uh-oh. She fell down. When you fell down what happened?"

Set the stage for your child to listen. Reduce background noise; turn off the television and radio. Choose a time and place where there will be minimal distractions and interruptions. Secure your child's attention first by calling her name, telling her to look at you, and bringing her close. Before reading together, point out important things so that she can listen for the main idea, both while listening to the text and during the conversation that accompanies the reading.

Make your verbal directions easy to follow. Use a normal, quiet voice to help your child feel calm and confident so he can listen without anxiety. Make each step short, clear, and simple to encourage careful listening (e.g., "Bring me four potatoes from the bag"). Accompany your instructions with opportunities for your child to practice the task. Have him repeat or explain back to you what you said, to make sure he understood. Even when we think we are being perfectly clear, our message can be misinterpreted; encourage him to ask for clarification, and praise him when he does.

Prepare your child for listening at school. Listening is more difficult for children when they are tired, hungry, or upset. Keep your child physically and emotionally ready to be a good listener at school. You will increase your child's school performance if you: organize and monitor her time, help her with homework, discuss school matters with her, and read with her (Finn 1998).

Sources: Based on Garman & Garman (1992); Konecki (1992).

- **They presented the task in more than one way, and gave Byron extra opportunities to absorb the information**—During the rehearsal, Byron's mom told him, "Hold the pillow right at your belly button." Later, when Byron appeared unsure of what to do, she demonstrated and told him, "Carry it carefully, out in front, like a plate of food to the dinner table."

- **They adjusted the pace so Byron had time to process the directions**—While the adults in the wedding party got their instructions verbally, practiced once or twice, and felt ready, the bridesmaids realized that Byron needed more time to help him process the directions and figure out his role. One walked with him down the aisle alone a few times, until he felt comfortable enough to rehearse it with the larger group.

- **They checked to make sure Byron understood what he was to do**—At the conclusion of the rehearsal, the group was asked if they had any questions. Byron whispered to his mom, "Where's the ring?" He knew what "ring bearer" meant but could not figure out why his little pillow was empty. His mother explained that on the real wedding day, the best man would place the ring on the pillow before Byron walked down the aisle.

- **The adults even assessed the experience**—As the group gathered after the ceremony for photos, the bride made sure to tell Byron that he had listened well and had done exactly what he was supposed to do. When she asked him if he had fun, he smiled and gave an enthusiastic "Yes!"

In situations such as these, the goal is *listening fidelity*—a match between our ideas and the child's understanding after the conversation (Powers & Bodie 2003). When listening fidelity occurs, the speakers and the listeners all share the same impression of how the conversation went and they arrive at a shared understanding of the material.

Answering questions about listening

We can be a resource to families in many ways if they need help to provide a rich home listening environment. One way we can help is by using our knowledge of research on how young children develop to answer parents' questions. Here are some common listening questions, and some of the research that can inform our answers:

"Why bother to talk to a baby who can't speak yet?"

Talking to young children from birth is important, and families differ greatly in how much they talk to their infants. From their earliest days, babies are learning about how conversations work as they interact with caring adults. Babies use facial expressions, gestures, and body posture (e.g., leaning forward) to imitate adults' nonverbal behavior during a conversation. These physical responses, in addition to babies' vocalizations (which are not yet words), prepare them for talk, just as surely as sitting up leads to standing up.

Listening is a major way of building vocabulary in very young children (Floor & Akhtar 2006; Jucszyk 2000). Toddlers understand speech long before they can speak themselves. When parents and infants do something together—eating, shopping, taking a walk, visiting a relative—the adult should talk about what they are doing, even though the child cannot yet reply (Armbruster, Lehr, & Osborn 2003). If they do this regularly, by the time a child is 18 months old, families will have spoken millions of words in the child's presence (Cruger 2005). Hearing language is a major factor in learning to speak it, and later on to read and write it.

"I ask my child questions all the time, but he barely answers me. How can I get him to talk more?"

When two adults want to strike up a conversation, they usually begin by trying to find a topic of shared interest. This strategy is equally important when conversing with a child. A young child is more likely to participate in talk if that individual child's interests, moods, expectations, personality, level of comfort, and level of understanding are taken into account. Consider this successful approach:

> A very shy 4-year-old visited a neighbor's home with her father. There, they met two women, one a teacher and the other a children's librarian. Sensing that the child was shy, the women did not draw attention to the child; instead, they spoke with the child's father in a relaxed way about some things the child might like to do while she was visiting. When she heard them mention an art kit, the preschooler excitedly asked the women, "Does it have markers?" Within a few moments, the child was

happily drawing and talking with the adults she had just met. As her father left, he told the adults, "I can tell that the two of you really know kids. I've never seen her warm up to new people like that. Now I see a better way to build her confidence. All along, I've been warning everyone that she's timid. But then people make an extra effort to ask her questions, she gets uncomfortable, and she really clams up. Thanks for finding a way to help her open up!"

An observational study of children whose language development lagged behind that of their peers found that in conversations with their children, parents commonly talked too much, monopolized the conversation, or focused on their own agenda. The researchers suggested that (1) engaging in conversation helps children to use language in a more efficient, effective, and concise manner; (2) parents may need special coaching to change their conversation habits; and (3) giving the child a few extra seconds to think about a response before the adult speaks (called "wait time") led to longer conversations (McNeill & Fowler 1996). Experts recommend a period of uninterrupted, one-to-one interaction with a child each day. Ward (2001), for example, recommends parent and child spend 30 minutes daily playing together quietly, during which they converse about something that reflects the child's interests.

"I've heard that listening to classical music enriches the brain. Is that true?"

This so-called "Mozart effect" has not been reliably demonstrated by research (Crncec, Wilson, & Prior 2006), although playing music in the background can be soothing. Instead, very young children learn best through active experiences. For example, in one study, 6- to 9-month-old infants were each videotaped with their mother while she sang a song, read a book aloud, played with a toy, or listened to recorded music. The researcher found the infants were most physically responsive when their mother read a book or played with a toy. Infants responded vocally to the toy, and older infants vocalized more than younger ones. The researcher concluded that singing, reading, and playing were far more effective in sustaining infant attention than recorded music was, possibly because talk about objects provides an opportunity for shared experiences (De l'Etoile 2006).

While listening to instrumental music certainly has its place, listening to lyrics is equally, if not more important for the very young.

Learning to Listen, Listening to Learn

Listening to words set to music can build listening skills, enhance abstract thinking, improve memory, and encourage the use of compound words, rhymes, and images (Hill-Clarke & Robinson 2004). Games, rhymes, and board books that incorporate singing, such as *Head, Shoulders, Knees, and Toes* (Kubler) support young children in their listening to music, and by extension, in their listening skills overall.

"I don't have time to read aloud. Can't my child get all the listening she needs from television and videos?"

The typical American child watches 21 hours of television per week (American Academy of Pediatrics 2007). Unfortunately, watching TV or videos is not a good substitute for being read to, primarily because watching is typically not as interactive as reading together. Listening to stories read aloud exercises mental skills that are the most similar to those required in reading independently. That is why a family who shares books at home with a child is the best predictor of the child's reading achievement in school (Anderson et al. 1985).

Television and videos aren't generally as intellectually challenging as a book because they "fill in the blanks" more than a book. Children don't listen or respond to television or videos as much as they simply look at them. No one needs a remedial course in TV watching; much of the time we can follow a TV program even with the sound turned off—using no listening skills at all.

Interpreting a book, on the other hand, calls upon children's prior knowledge and resources. We see these differences in processing images versus print in studies that, for example, ask children to retell stories. When they retell a story they have watched, they tend to focus on action and use lots of verbs. But when children retell stories from picture books, they use more new vocabulary—picked up from the author—and pay more attention to the sounds of language (Haden, Ornstein, & Didow 2001).

We can, however, reassure parents that watching television or videos isn't all bad, with a few caveats. The television should be off at mealtimes, as these are prime opportunities for the entire family to exercise their oral language skills in conversation. Parents can be selective about their young child's viewing habits and influence them to watch some programs that have a literacy tie-in, such as *Reading*

Rainbow or *Between the Lions*. After they find something suitable for a young child, adult and child can watch it together and talk about it afterwards.

Talking is key. Whether watching a children's television program or listening to a picture book, children learn the most from having the adult clarify, interpret, and query what is seen or read ("Why did she do that?" "Was it a good or bad idea?" "Would you have done the same?"). The thing about reading aloud that makes the greatest impression on children—even children as young as 2 or 3—is what is discussed with the parent (Haden, Ornstein, & Didow 2001).

"Doesn't supporting my child's language growth at home require training or special materials?"

Frank Smith (2003), a leading authority on literacy, points out that children learn to read through positive relationships with people who support their efforts: "Helping a child to become a reader requires no special materials or techniques, only vastly important and precious qualities of patience, tolerance, empathy, and sensitivity. Children learn to read by reading, provided they are interested in what they read and not confused by it" (17). Parents who read aloud to their child, for example, exert a positive influence on that child's emotions and motivation to become literate when they arrange the physical environment (e.g., find a quiet time and a comfortable place); bring literacy materials into the home (e.g., borrow books from the library); support interpersonal interactions (e.g., discuss the images and ideas in picture books); and model positive attitudes toward literacy (e.g., show enthusiasm for a bedtime story) (Braunger & Lewis 2005).

The things families routinely do—shop for groceries, sing in the car, send and receive messages, participate in celebrations, communicate with relatives—all can be opportunities to develop their young child's listening and speaking (oral language) skills (Nistler & Maiers 2000; Saracho 2002). For example, Saracho (2007) describes a father and his preschool son making peanut butter to spread on bread for a snack. They use magic markers to capture the recipe in pictures and words so they can do the activity together again. A pleasurable activity like this accomplishes much more language learning than 10 minutes of practice with vocabulary flashcards does, and no special equipment or expertise was needed. The recipe mattered to the boy and his father, so the learning was meaningful. Recording it demonstrated the utility of learning to read and write. And, perhaps most important of all, the father was a role model of enthusiasm for becoming literate—all outside a formal or academic setting.

Family listening activities

One way that teachers can support listening at home is by sharing with families some activities that promote active listening.

Everyday activities

Like the father and son's peanut butter recipe, everyday activities and simple games can support language development (see Dougherty & Paul 2007). When preparing a salad, for instance, parent and child can talk about the different types of vegetables and then start a guessing game—the child closes her eyes and listens to a carrot snap, then guesses what food item made the sound (Dougherty 1999).

Babies respond to the sounds their parents make and try to see where the noises are coming from. Interesting noises with toys or objects will also capture infants' attention and get them actively exploring the origins of the noise. Infants and toddlers can be encouraged to make their own noises or imitate some of the sounds they hear in stories and rhymes, such as animal sounds.

Another idea is for the parent to say several words that go together and one that does not (e.g., "*mittens, boots, teddy, scarf*"), then ask the child to identify the one that doesn't fit and say why. An activity that promotes listening and recall is to start a series and invite the child to add to it. For example, the mom might say, "When we go to the store, we'll get rice cakes and…"; if the child says, "oatmeal," mom would follow up with, "When we go to the store we'll get rice cakes, oatmeal, and…," and so on.

Special events

Here's an example where parents made a special event even more special, by adding new vocabulary to an already notable experience, a family trip to Belgium:

> While viewing a diorama of the Battle of Waterloo, which included a fallen soldier with his armor cast aside, 4-year-old Kaylan pointed and said, "There's that thing they wear so they don't get hurt." "Yes, *armor*," said his mother. When Kaylan's father walked up, Kaylan announced, "Look, it's armor!"

The following ideas work because they prompt listening and talking in order to plan, describe, select, record, and so on. Families can use special outings as the basis for making a personal scrapbook, with the child helping to create captions for each photo. A family activity suitable for older children is to create a family tree. Another is assembling a memory box of childhood, which begins with the parent selecting a special container and collecting representative items from the child's life, such as a favorite toy, an article of clothing, a photograph, a sample drawing or writing, and the like. From time to time the child can choose something and parent and child can tell stories about it. A recording of the child's voice could go in the box, too. The family can go back periodically and listen to the recordings, and talk about the progress the child is making.

Book discussions

Jenny's favorite picture book is *Baby Animals*, illustrated by Garth Williams. When the toddler looks at the book, she does not patiently turn each page. Instead, she immediately begins to search for the baby owl, makes a soft hooting noise when she sees it, and then she's done. If Jenny's parents tried to insist that she sit quietly and listen from beginning to end, they'd have a struggle on their hands. Fortunately, they are satisfied for the time being that she is interested in the book—even if only briefly. Their goal is to teach Jenny to associate pleasure with books; they know that later their reading sessions will get longer and more interactive as Jenny's attention span lengthens.

Here's a basic strategy for talking about books with young children that parents may appreciate; it uses the acronym SHARE:

Set up the environment for listening

Help the child to control the book and take the lead

Accept the child's responses

Relate the book to the child's life

Experience the book again if the child is still interested in it

Something else to share with parents is that children actually do learn a lot from repetition—although even *The Very Hungry Caterpillar* can get tiresome for the adult, no matter how gorgeous Eric Carle's illustrations are. Revisiting the same book until they have it memorized is frequently overlooked as an achievement in children's development, yet it is a major stride toward learning to read (Jalongo 2006). Gradually, children begin to pay attention to the print—not just the pictures—and figure out *word boundaries* (i.e., where one word begins and another ends). From memory, they can eventually "finger-point read" and match letters with sounds (Uhry 2002). As they gain more and more familiarity with the text, they tend to ask more sophisticated questions. Such questions lead to a deeper understanding of the text and form a strong foundation for reading comprehension.

Learning opportunities

Many parents admit that although they would like to be more involved, they do not know what they could be doing to help their child learn to read. In one study, 75 percent of parents said that they could help more if they were taught specific strategies (Cook-Cottone 2004). Not surprisingly, then, parents engaged in more literacy activities with their child when they were taught some simple techniques: (1) read aloud expressively; (2) ask "friendly," inviting questions; (3) encourage the child to guess what might happen next; and (4) share books in different ways, such as taking turns reading portions of the text or doing echo reading (Annett 2004; Cook-Cottone 2004). When families see their child enjoying books, they make more time for reading with the child (see Darling & Westberg 2004).

Storytelling

Often we are better able to understand and remember information if it is presented in story form. Groce (2004) notes, "Storytelling has a

Benefits of Storytelling

Many benefits accrue from both telling and listening to oral stories:

- Listening to storytelling improves children's listening comprehension, a vital prereading skill; and it develops their mental imaging ability, a skill necessary for reading comprehension.

- The pleasure that children get from listening to storytelling helps them to associate listening with enjoyment while it teaches them to be respectful listeners, enhances vocabulary, and assists them in discovering the beauty and power of words (Bishop & Kimball 2006).

- Each family has its own stories passed down through the generations. Listening to and engaging with family stories—such as those told around the dinner table—have been shown to improve children's oral language and literacy development (Groce 2004). Family stories also make a major contribution to a child's sense of self. Young children develop a sense of identity and their place within a family by discussing personally significant events. When no one shares and revisits family stories, the autobiographical memories of childhood are not as well formed (Nelson 2007).

- When children tell a story, it provides a glimpse into their higher-level cognitive processes, their representations of themselves, their understandings of the task, and their inferences about the listeners (Nelson, Aksu-Koc, & Johnson 2001).

- Asking children to retell a familiar story is a good way to check their understanding of and emerging ideas about the concept of plot. Storytelling also helps English language learners begin to note similarities between their first language and English while helping their academic achievement in school, particularly in the language arts (Mason & Au 1998).

long tradition of orally communicating ideas, beliefs, personal histories, and life-lessons. Most children begin hearing and telling stories before they enter school or learn to read and write" (122).

Why and how families tell stories is an expression of a group's culture. In some cultures, oral storytelling ability is valued as much or more than literacy with print is (Barone & Morrow 2002). Storytelling styles also differ among cultures. Awareness of these differences in storytelling styles and preferences can help teachers to move beyond those favored by the dominant group, thereby making the curriculum more responsive to diverse learners. For example, European Americans tend to tell stories with a single topic focus and a definite beginning, middle, and end; African Americans tend to include more than one topic, flow freely from one event to the next, emphasize personal meaning and engagement, and use more figurative language (Bloome et al. 2001; Hale-Benson 1986).

Extra resources

To support listening and literacy, families can borrow books, music recordings, audiobooks, and videos of children's books from the child's school or public library. Community bulletin boards announce listening events, often free and sponsored by the local library, such as Story Hour, presentations by professional storytellers, puppet shows, and other read-aloud events (Cook-Cottone 2004).When parents of children with communication difficulties use such activities, they have more positive attitudes about helping their child, and children's listening skills improve (Stevens, Watson, & Dodd 2001).

Conclusion

During a parent-teacher conference, the preschool teacher shared with a mother what her daughter had told the group the week before. The family dog had gotten out of the fenced yard and had run around the neighborhood. "Did somebody accidentally leave the gate open?" the teacher had asked. The 4-year-old had answered, "Well, *evidently*, he knows how to open the gate all by himself." The teacher wanted the mother to know how impressed he was by her child's vocabulary. To which the child's mother replied, "I don't know where Heather gets that stuff. Evidently, she…" With that, both mother and teacher smiled, realizing simultaneously that it was very clear where the word had come from!

Just as this child picked up her mother's favorite word, so do children pick up the listening attitudes, skills, and habits practiced in the home. As with most of the important life lessons that children learn, those demonstrated by example are a powerful influence on a young child's behavior. When we help families provide their children with rich, supportive, developmentally appropriate listening environments, we are playing an important role in making the child a better listener and learner.

Chapter 6

Teachers as Listeners

Becoming an effective listener is an exciting and rewarding experience. It is only fair to emphasize, however, that improving listening abilities is difficult, demanding, and challenging.

—James Floyd

On a long, cross-country flight, a boy who appeared to be about 7 years old and a silver-haired woman chatted nonstop, their gestures and facial expressions showing that both were enjoying the conversation thoroughly. As the passengers began lining up to exit the aircraft, a man said to the boy, "You and your grandma can go ahead," to which the woman replied, "Well, thank you very much, but this nice young man is not my grandson. We had the pleasure of getting acquainted during the trip." I could not resist asking, was she a teacher? She answered, with quiet pride, "Yes, I taught elementary school for 37 years, but now I am retired." This veteran teacher clearly had mastered the art of conversing with a young child.

Learning how to interact verbally with young children is no small accomplishment. Adults need to take a great share of the responsibility for successful communication when interacting with a young child.

> [By] directing attention, organizing and structuring the time course
> of the conversation, storing information to compensate for the child's

weaker working memory, reminding, monitoring, and prompting…
[the adult] facilitates and supports the child's language production
and, at the same time, models listening behavior. (Imhof 2002, 42)

We demonstrate interest, care, and concern when we take the time
to explore ideas with children, allow children time to collect their
thoughts, exercise care about what we say directly to a child or
within a child's hearing (Shidler-Lattz 2002), and respond not only
to children's words but also to the feelings that underlie those words
(Gartrell 2006).

Listening is also a way to support the goals of inclusion. Effective teachers listen "across differences" (Schultz 2003). Through
thoughtful listening they get to know each child a little bit better,
becoming aware of the social and cultural forces in that child's life.
Teachers who listen effectively are tuned into the rhythm and balance of the classroom, so they recognize situations that could silence
or exclude in time to intervene (Schultz 2003).

Listening and being listened to are major ways we all build and
sustain relationships, and not only with children (Purdy 2006). Few
people will admit that they are poor listeners, yet most of us have a
long list of complaints about the listening habits of others. Whether it
is wives and husbands, parents and teachers, bosses and employees,
or coworkers, those who are being listened to are seldom satisfied.

The listening habits and styles of teachers

Early childhood educator and founder of the Reggio Emilia schools,
Loris Malaguzzi, contends that we teach children to listen by being
good listeners ourselves (NAEYC 1994). The question is: Are we
models of good listening?

Before becoming teachers, every one of us has accumulated
thousands of hours as a student. If our own education was typical,
between 65 and 90 percent of our in-school time was spent listening
(Gilbert 2005), mostly to teacher talk. "All evidence from research
tells us that, in most classrooms, the range of opportunities for learners to contribute to talk is quite narrow and the amount of talk they
contribute is relatively small" (Mercer 1995, 60). In other words, our
own time as students may have ingrained in us the lesson that the

Learning to Listen, Listening to Learn

Are You a Good Listener?

Do you consider yourself to be a good listener? Try this activity to find out more about your listening skills:

Assemble in groups of three. One person will be the listener, one the speaker, and one the observer. The speaker will talk for three minutes without interruption (other than for clarification) about the most innovative thing she or he has done in teaching all year. The listener will attempt to practice all of the LADDERS skills. The observer will evaluate the listener by using the LADDERS list below and jotting down observations:

LADDERS to Active Listening

Look at the person you are talking with and use body language to express your interest.

Ask pertinent questions and make relevant comments after the speaker has finished.

Don't interrupt or allow yourself to become distracted. Keep asking yourself, "What's the point?"

Don't change the subject. Make a brief mental summary of the conversation as you go along. Take notes if it will help you to remember, but do not allow them to interfere with the communication.

Emotions should be kept under control. Try to identify with the speaker.

Respond appropriately to words and underlying meanings.

Slow down your internal thoughts and concentrate on the speaker's message (Gregg 1983).

Now change roles. After three more minutes, change roles again, so that each person has a turn in the listener's role. When the activity is finished, use the self-assessment below to evaluate how you behaved when you were the listener.

Listener's Self-Assessment

- Did three minutes seem like a long time to listen attentively?
- Was I able to resist distractions, or did my attention wane?
- Did I avoid judging the speaker, attending to her habits or mannerisms, reacting to particular words, or jumping to conclusions?
- Did I find myself thinking about what I might say, rather than focusing on what the speaker was saying?
- Did I listen "between the lines," taking in not only the explicit messages but also the implicit ones?

After completing the self-assessment, compare and contrast it with the observer's notes on your listening behavior.

Source: Based on Vining & Yrle (1980).

teacher's role is to talk and children's role is to listen—exactly the *opposite* of Malaguzzi's advice. Because teachers tend to "deliver lessons using the same structure their instructors used to teach them" (Gilbert 2005, 1), we may have to "unlearn" that lesson before we can become the model listeners that children in our classrooms need us to be.

As described in Chapter 1, *effective listening* means the listener takes in the message accurately and interprets it appropriately. Effective listeners also adapt quickly to particular listening contexts and situations (Imhof 2004). For example, teachers who are effective listeners listen differently depending on whether they are studying, talking with family or friends, planning with colleagues, or interacting with a professional from another field.

Listening is influenced by context, but many adults also have a preferred listening style, defined as a set of "attitudes, beliefs, and predispositions about the how, where, when, who, and what of the information reception and encoding process" (Watson, Barker, & Weaver 1995, 2). About 40 percent of listeners have one strong style to which they resort—especially when under pressure or in situations where they feel unsure; about another 40 percent have no set preference (Barker & Watson 2000). Acknowledging the following listening styles can help us as we examine our own skills and challenges:

- **People-oriented** listeners are interested in demonstrating concern for others' emotions and interests, finding common ground, and responding.

- **Action-oriented** listeners are interested in direct, concise, error-free communication that is used to negotiate and accomplish a goal; these listeners are easily frustrated by disorganized presentations.

- **Content-oriented** listeners are interested in intellectual challenge and complex information; they want to carefully evaluate information before forming judgments and opinions.

- **Time-oriented** listeners prefer brief communication; such listeners seek interaction that is concise and to the point, and they desire to know the length of time available before the communication begins.

Research into adult listening styles suggests that people rate themselves as better listeners than their peers judge them to be; gender stereotypes often cause peers to rate females as *people-oriented* and males as *action-oriented,* even when they are not. A country's dominant culture or subgroups within a country may tend to prefer a particular style. For example, several studies found that young adults in America lean toward the *people-oriented* style, in which the goal is to find common ground and express concern through listening (Barker & Watson 2000; Kiewitz et al. 1997; Sargent & Weaver 2003; Timm & Schroeder 2000). We may have a different listening style outside of the classroom, but in the classroom, many teachers gravitate toward the *action-* and *time-oriented* styles.

About 80 percent of teachers' interaction in classrooms is task-oriented: Teachers tend to give instructions (e.g., "Everyone hold your paper this way"), supply information (e.g., "All of these animals lay eggs"), or make corrections (e.g., "This is a *b*, not a *d*"). Approximately 80 percent of teachers' task-oriented talk consists of low-level questions that require children to recall some bit of information (Kerry 1982), instead of teacher talk that emphasizes higher-level questions that move beyond remembering information.

The typical teacher/child verbal exchange in many classrooms consists of the teacher's question, the child's short reply, and a quick teacher assessment of whether or not the response meets the teacher's expectations. This traditional pedagogy—in which we are dispensers of information and students are passive recipients—is an approach we all should use less often in the classroom, preschool through graduate school. Consider this example:

> On the first sunny day after a long winter, a preschool class gathered for their morning circle time. After the children sang a weather song, the teacher displayed the class weather chart and asked, "Tamika, what is the weather today?" Tamika looked out the window, smiled, and said excitedly, "Spring!" The teacher replied, "No. It has to be one of the weather symbols: *windy, rainy, cloudy, sunny,* or *snowy.*"

Tamika's response was not wrong; it just wasn't what the teacher wanted to hear. Williams (1992) explains what happens when teachers rush to evaluate a child's response:

> The pupil who appears most able is the one who is most successful at guessing the framework within which the teacher is operating, the one

who guesses what it is that the teacher really wants to know. What the teacher cannot tell from these kinds of interactions is how well individual children are able to use their oral language to show what they are really understanding. (111)

A better a listening response would have been for that teacher to say, "Yes, it does feel like spring today. Which weather symbol will you choose for the calendar?" The way we receive children's responses communicates expectations to them about what and how language can and should be used (Pantaleo 2007).

What if a child's contribution to a discussion is a factual error, such as when a child misinterprets a story the class is reading? Many teachers feel it is their responsibility to step in and correct the error. Instead, Aukerman (2006) finds that:

> [The] teacher's refusal to judge their ideas as right or wrong enabled the students to share responsibility for closely evaluating their own and one another's ideas.... Taking students' ideas seriously—even when those ideas seem tangential, unsupported, or incomprehensible...means following up on precisely those ideas that most puzzle you, engaging students with one another's ideas, and monitoring your impulse to bring things back to the ideas that you consider most important. (40–41)

Really listening to children

Despite all the benefits of really seeing and hearing children,

> as teachers we are often ambivalent about the talk that goes on in our classrooms. We want it, and yet we don't.... But what do we make of the talk that eludes our control, that slips into the territories for which we have not planned? Is it important? Is it noise? Or is it talk, communication? (Salyer 1994, 42)

Children know when we are not really listening to them, just like they know when we skip pages while reading their favorite picture book. Children pay particular attention to overt signs of attentive listening. Imhof (2002), for example, asks elementary school children what a person who listens well (and poorly) does:

- Children's top five criteria for judging someone a *good* listener are that the person (1) makes eye contact appropriately, (2) is patient and does not interrupt, (3) asks questions in a nonthreatening tone, (4) is responsive both verbally and nonverbally, and (5) prepares for listening.

Do You Listen to All Kinds of Children?

Ask yourself these questions to help you reflect on your habits as a listener in an inclusive classroom:

- How do I deal with children who seldom talk or are very soft-spoken? Do I encourage them to remain quiet to keep the level of children's talk in the classroom low, or do I make a genuine attempt to draw them into conversation?

- How do I deal with children who are exceptionally talkative or loud? Do I make assumptions about them and their families? Do my assumptions differ based on gender, race, or culture?

- Do I listen patiently to children who have difficulty expressing their ideas and struggle to be understood, or do I quickly move on? Do I make opportunities for them to be heard, not only by me but also by their peers?

- What do I do when children who have asked for a chance to speak fall silent when their turn comes? Am I sensitive to the fact that young children can forget what they were about to say, and do I ensure they have another chance to speak?

- How about when children's behavior is challenging—does everyone get treated fairly, or does the child skilled in verbal expression (e.g., a "smooth talker") avoid consequences more often?

- Do I ask many different types of questions, allowing more children chances to contribute, or do I play the "read the teacher's mind" game much of the time?

- When children say something of questionable accuracy, how do I handle it? Do I pounce on the statement as a "lie," or do I try to get further clarification? If I know it to be untrue or inaccurate, do I lose respect for the child, or remember that the line between fantasy and reality for young children is a dotted one? Do I consider that children sometimes express wishes as fact, and acknowledge this sensitively, with a comment such as, "Yes, wouldn't it be nice if we could … "

- How do I respond if a child shares something that makes me uncomfortable (e.g., "My cat got runned over by a car" … "My dad promised to take me camping, but I waited all weekend and he never came to get me"). Do I quickly move on, or do I acknowledge the feelings that underlie the message ("It is so sad to lose our pets" … "You were upset that a promise was broken")?

Interestingly, children identify *friends* and *grandparents* as their favorite listeners (two groups often willing to give more of their time).

- Children's criteria for judging someone a *poor* listener are that the person (1) does not make eye contact, (2) is not focused on the message being conveyed, (3) is too busy or preoccupied to listen, (4) is not interested, and (5) gives little or no verbal or nonverbal feedback.

Children and adults give very similar answers, except that children rate someone a good listener if he or she prepares for listening (e.g., turns off the television, invites the child to cuddle); whereas adults are more concerned about a listener being open-minded and non-judgmental (Imhof 2002).

Children need us to listen to them. As such, they can best judge whether or not we have been listening effectively. We can best meet children's need to be heard if, when we evaluate our own listening skills, we take into consideration children's thoughts on what makes a good listener.

Listening to parents/families

Life for young children is shaped by relationships. To thrive, children need settings where all the important adults in their lives care about them and about each other. At the minimum, a child needs family and teacher to share information and coordinate their efforts. But beyond the practical, children feel more "listened to" when relationships between their families and their teachers are warm, collaborative, and respectful. When there is a positive relationship between family and teacher, the benefits are many: teachers feel comfortable bonding with children, children get seamless care, teachers feel rewarded, parents relax, and both become more trusting and tolerant of the other (Baker & Manfredi/Petitt 2004). When the adults who care for a child aren't listening to each other, it is the child who suffers most (Gonzalez-Mena 1998; Kendall 1996).

Failure to communicate is a serious detriment to any relationship; conversely, really listening to another person is a powerful relationship-building tool. "Connecting with others is at the heart of communication—defined best as one person understanding what

Is Your Thinking a Barrier to Listening?

Talking too much—"If I do all the talking, you'll go along with my thinking."

Talking too little—"If I say nothing, I can end this conversation."

Judging—"I'm in the right."

Blaming—"You're in the wrong."

Preoccupation with self—"You ought to think/feel/behave as I expect."

Topping—"You won't believe what happened to *me*."

Defensiveness—"It's not my fault."

Counterattack—"How dare you criticize me. You're not perfect."

Denial—"Problem? What problem?"

Diverting—"I'll never forget the day they…"

Assuming—"I know exactly how you feel."

Advising—"I know just what you should do."

Control—"I need to be in charge."

Helplessness—"It is what it is."

———

Source: Based on Burns (1999).

another wants understood. The key to this understanding is listening" (Gilbert 2005, 2). Awareness of other people's feelings and mood states is essential, both in effective listening and in empathy (Bommelje, Houston, & Smither 2003). At its most sophisticated levels, listening is combined with empathy so that we can discern another person's thoughts and feelings with some degree of accuracy and listen on an intuitive as well as a literal level (Comer & Drollinger 1999). The box *above* identifies thinking that gets in the way of our listening to families.

The kind of empathetic listening that parents and other family members often need from early childhood educators is *reflective listening*, which differs from ordinary listening in four important ways. Reflective listening means the listener: (1) listens thoughtfully to the meaning of the speaker's words; (2) considers the content of the message, both stated and implied; (3) thinks about the feelings associated with the message, attending to the speaker's verbal and nonverbal cues; and (4) makes every effort to reflect that message back accurately. For example,

> A mother and father attend a parent conference. The mother says, "Our son is not doing well in reading. This really worries us because my husband struggled for years with reading until he found out he was dyslexic."

How should the teacher respond? Many ineffective listening responses arise from a certain level of discomfort with discussing difficult issues such as this one. Sometimes, teachers attempt to gloss over concerns out of a false sense of being "nice." So, a teacher might dismiss the parents' concerns (e.g., "Oh, his reading is not that bad") or change the subject ("He's doing well in math, though") rather than respond to the concern. Such responses leave the parents feeling that their worries are unacknowledged and unimportant. Instead, a reflective listening response—one that communicates understanding—might be,

> "It sounds as though you have been worrying that your son could be dyslexic and wondering what can be done to prevent him from having the same kind of struggles that your husband experienced as a child."

This type of response opens the door to further discussion because the parents' concerns have been recognized. Reflective listening truly encourages the speaker—it "heartens" and "emboldens." Feeling validated, parents might continue with, "We just want to do everything possible to prevent reading problems," a goal with which the teacher can affiliate:

> "As a teacher, that is my goal too. Your son can benefit from more experiences with books. There are many resources we can use to help. I'll be sending home some collections of picture books you can share. I also have information about the free preschool story time at the public library."

As teachers gain practice with reflective listening, they realize that it is a way of demonstrating care, concern, and support while inviting more dialogue with families.

Additional strategies

Here are some additional strategies for communicating effectively with parents/families:

Show cultural sensitivity. Discrimination, prejudice, and stereotyping interfere with effective communication, and certainly have no place in an early childhood setting. Less malevolent but still damaging to communication between teachers and families is ignorance of or insensitivity to a child's home culture. Knowing something about a child's religion, for example, is one way to help us better know the child and prevent cultural insensitivity. We need, at the very least, to respect and have a basic understanding of children's belief systems (and to show similar respect if children are not part of any religious tradition). It is also essential to teach children to respect their classmates' religions. It may even be helpful to familiarize children with certain key elements (such as holidays, styles of dress, etc.), which will make them more sensitive to those around them (Couchenour & Chrisman 2003; Hoot, Szecsi, & Moosa 2003). As Timm and Schroeder (2000) note:

> To communicate with diverse groups, individuals need to become knowledgeable about these diverse cultures, including their communication patterns, especially in relation to listening/nonverbal communication.... Individuals who are more competent intercultural communicators tend to be more multiculturally sensitive. (110, 113)

Ask questions that matter. Ask parents/families about their hopes and dreams for their child—you may be surprised. Sometimes their goals are related to school readiness, such as the goals of these parents of a preschooler: "We just want her to learn her letters and numbers and how to write a little bit." At other times, their hopes for their children have more to do with social and emotional development. New to the United States, these parents from Bangladesh had an important goal for their kindergartner: "If only she could have just one little friend to eat lunch with." Include parents in thoroughly discussing the curriculum. Ask them what the school/program is doing that is right for their child; ask them what could be improved. Ask them how they prefer to communicate with the school and what makes them feel heard and respected.

Meet frustration and anger with calm. Parents sometimes use language in ways that can make teachers feel unappreciated. If a parent says, "I attended that meeting about the new writing program, but it was a big waste of time," a teacher's impulse may be defensive: "Well, I think it was a great program." It is better simply to let parents know you heard the message (reflective listening), and keep the tone positive. You might say, "Evidently the meeting didn't have much value for you. Do you have any suggestions for what would make it more helpful?" When we talk with parents, even distraught or angry parents, we need to use the same tone and manner as we would use with a highly esteemed colleague. Do not meet frustration and anger with your frustration and anger; the more intense the situation becomes, the calmer *you* need to become.

Use "feel/felt/found." Another way to hear a critical message without becoming defensive is to use a strategy called "feel/felt/found" (Garmston 2005). First, accept the feelings expressed by the person (this is the "feel" part):

> "Many people feel as you do…"

Next, identify with the concern personally (this is the "felt" part):

> "I used to have some of those same worries and felt that way, too…"

Finally, show how your ideas have been changed (this is the "found" part):

> "But now that I have worked with many, many young children, I have found…"

Showing this progression of thought is a more effective way to defuse a situation than blurting out, "I disagree!"

Focus on the one big thing. When negotiating an issue with parents, try to determine what the major sticking point is. If you can yield on that "one big thing," do so. If not, explain why you cannot. If, for example, a parent wants you to use corporal punishment, you might say, "I understand what you are saying, but it is against our school rules and the laws in this country for teachers to hit a child. We will have to find another way, a way to encourage good behavior rather than punish misbehavior."

Don't reject the parent. When a parent tells us something that is problematic but important to know, keeping the lines of communication open takes priority. That was the situation here:

> A preschooler who was obviously terrified crawled under the desk and lashed out at anyone who came near. No one could figure out what was going on with this 4-year-old until her teenage mother said, "We watch really scary slasher movies together because I'm afraid to watch them alone. Do you think that's a bad idea?"

Rather than chastising or isolating this young mother for hurting her daughter, the teacher said, "Since you asked the question, it sounds as though you suspect that these movies might be frightening to your child. I agree with you. You should stop having her watch those movies." If, instead, the teacher had jumped to criticize, this parent probably would not have asked such a question again, and the teacher would have lost an important source of insight into the child's home life.

Be responsible with what you hear. In the interest of effective communication, teachers (and parents) have to agree to behave responsibly with what we hear young children say—and they do say the darnedest things. Here are two situations that called for tact and calm from all involved:

> On her first day of first grade, a child said to her teacher, "Remember me from kindergarten? If you don't recognize me, it's because I got my hair cut. It used to be really long—all the way down to my butt. I got it cut the same day my dad shaved off his beard. My mom said she wouldn't sleep with him anymore if he didn't shave it off."

The teacher imagined correctly that this first-grader's parents would not want their personal business broadcasted, and she took care not to repeat what she heard to other teachers in the program. Empathy—putting ourselves in the other person's shoes—is key in keeping parents and teachers listening to each other. In the next example, the parent checked out what he heard, saving the teacher from being accused of mistreating children:

> When a father asked, "What did you do at child care today?" his preschool daughter replied, in disgust, "They made us eat dirt and worms." The father was skeptical, so the next day at drop-off he asked her teacher about it. As it turned out, another parent had brought a "dirt cake" to the class picnic—a clean flowerpot filled with ground-up Oreo cookie "dirt" and Gummy Worms.

Identify with parents/families. A program's failure to commit to effective communication undermines the collaboration necessary to support children's learning. In this example, the school may have thought it was communicating with the family, but the father's reaction implies something different about what messages were being heard:

> The parents of a second-grader were asked to come to school to discuss their son's academic performance. When they arrived, they

were shocked and surprised to hear that his reading skills were far below those of his peers, and that the school was recommending support services. The presence of the principal, the classroom teacher, the reading specialist, and an instructional support team teacher made the parents feel outnumbered. As the team began suggesting how the parents could help at home, the father interrupted angrily, "Teaching him to read is your job! This is the first I've heard about serious reading problems. Why weren't we told about this sooner?"

Such outbursts are apt to occur when parents feel that educators have not adequately communicated with them. It may also be that what the teachers intend as a discussion of the child's difficulties with reading, the parents perceive as criticism of them and their parenting skills. This situation illustrates the communication breakdowns that occur when educators exercise power over parents and families with little attention to the parents' perspectives. Clearly, too, the father's reaction will make future communication between home and school more difficult and strained, as it goes against many of the commonsense principles for effective listening.

Effective programs recognize the importance of developmentally appropriate practice for "establishing reciprocal relationships

---

Commonsense Communicating

According to experts, the best ways to promote effective communication don't change:

- Try to put the other person at ease. Use reflective listening strategies, and if possible, empathize with the speaker.

- Demonstrate your willingness to listen by withholding judgment until you've heard the other person out.

- Be patient and persist in trying to understand the speaker's message.

- Keep your own emotions under control.

- Be very slow to disagree, criticize, argue, or interrupt. Try asking questions instead.

- Resist distractions, and try to concentrate on the central ideas. Take notes if it helps.

- Strive to find areas of agreement, or "common ground."

Sources: Nichols & Stevens (1957a; 1957b); Wolvin (2006).

Learning to Listen, Listening to Learn

with families" (NAEYC 1997), and they actively seek input from parents and other family members (Bushman & Buster 2002). There are numerous ways we can ensure that family input is heard:

- **Home visits.** Some programs ask to conduct home visits to get a sense of children's family, cultural, and community backgrounds.

- **Mailings.** Schools, programs, and districts often send home requests for information in the form of questionnaires. Calendars of important events let families know about scheduled opportunities to be heard in person.

- **Group interviews.** Programs sometimes collect feedback on an issue by asking a representative group of parents to participate in a group interview or focus group.

- **Regular communications.** Programs should know how families prefer to keep in touch (in-person meetings, telephone conversations, quick exchanges at pickup or drop-off, notes, emails, etc.), and they should communicate often.

- **Evaluations of materials.** Many programs loan out materials that children can take home, such as books and audiotapes. Often the parent is asked to complete a brief evaluation card, to learn which materials were more and less useful.

- **Parent-teacher conferences.** These are the oldest and most common opportunities for families to interact with their child's teacher. (For more about conferencing, see Seplocha 2007.)

Listening to our colleagues

When communication breaks down, it can disrupt and sometimes do permanent damage to professional relationships. That is what happened between a supervising teacher and her supervisee:

"My student teacher was responsible for bringing insects to kindergarten class so that the children could observe them. I told her about this well in advance and made arrangements for her to get the insects from the high school biology teacher. I also reminded her about it. The day before our theme on insects was to begin, I asked if she had picked them up and she said no. I said, 'Well, then, you are going to be busy after school today because I am not disappointing the children.' To her credit, by the next morning she had gathered enough insects on her own for the children to observe with their magnifying glasses and begin their journals. But why didn't she listen to me?"

As a result of this event, each teacher lowered her opinion of the other: The student teacher felt her mentor teacher had "turned on her," and the mentor teacher felt her student teacher was irresponsible. Within a few weeks, the student teacher had withdrawn from the program, saying that she was too stressed to continue.

As it did in this example, when we fail to listen to the explicit and implicit messages our colleagues send us, it can result in embarrassment, costly mistakes, hurt feelings, diminished professional effectiveness, and worse. Poor listening skills in the workplace can have significant consequences, which helps to explain why businesses invest in listening training (Burley-Allen 1995). They know that listening is a key to effective leadership (Steil & Bommelje 2004). "Employees feel more valued when their supervisors listen to their opinions, and we trust people who listen to us" (Bentley 2000, 139). Interestingly, when 2,000 businesspeople were asked to draw a caricature of a successful, value-driven leader, 90 percent drew large ears, a big heart, or both:

> The message is clear: Effective leaders hear what others have to say and empathize with their issues....People perceive a lack of empathy because those around them don't take the time to find out what they are feeling—and, yes, don't take the time to listen. So, these two characteristics—caring and feeling—are very much intertwined. Effective leaders listen empathetically. (Lucia 1997, 25)

Research tells us that listening with empathy is the basis for a host of important workplace skills and strategies—assessing situations, making rational decisions, generating connections between theory and practice, arriving at deeper understandings about beliefs, adapting to new perspectives, informing instructional decisions, challenging traditions, improving teaching and learning, and validating ideals (Black 2001; Ferraro 2000; Conderman & Morin 2004; Risko, Roskos, & Vukelich 2002). Leaders who know the value of listening will emphasize collegiality and colleagues listening to one another.

Listening also can be a useful tool for reflecting with your colleagues. The following group activity is adapted from Conderman and Morin (2004) and Kamp (2006).

To set a context for the reflection, begin from some shared assumptions:

- All of us are engaged in learning from one another. We are bound by a responsibility, not only to further our own learning but also to help all members of the community learn effectively.

- Learning requires a mutual effort in helping one another understand the differing points of view we may bring to a topic, issue, or situation.

- It is important to stay in communication even when we are confused or fearful or unsure because this is the only way to explore appropriate solutions to problems.

- Learning begins by relating information, events, and perspectives to our previous learning, backgrounds, and experiences; it then moves into applying newly acquired insights to the current circumstances.

- A mature individual has learned that "understanding" does not imply *agreement*. It is possible to disagree and critique without rancor, hostility, or personal attacks.

Next, consider these questions about listening, discussing them as a group:

- Why is listening different today than the way it was years ago?

- What are some things that make it difficult to listen?

- In reviewing our curriculum, where is the teaching of listening skills evident?

- What have we done to improve our skills as listeners?

- How has technology affected listening in the educational context?

- How do we decide the best way to communicate (face-to-face, telephone, email, etc.) with various stakeholders?

- What measures do we take to include everyone in the process and communicate effectively with diverse speakers and listeners?

Finally, try some of these reflective listening exercises:

- Conference with a colleague about why she pursued a teaching career, her pivotal influences, and what has kept her in the profession.

- Switch roles; temporarily accept an assignment that a colleague normally has but one that you could do comfortably. Discuss how your usual roles overlap and ways that communication between the two of you could benefit children.

- Copy and share with the group an educational issue covered in the newspaper; a pithy, thought-provoking quotation; or online discussion group posting to stimulate dialogue (and perhaps debate).

- Reflect on your teaching day or a particularly challenging situation, being careful to protect confidentiality. Share your reflection with a trusted colleague or mentor, and discuss.

- Describe a significant change that you have made in your teaching, what prompted the change, and its results.

Conclusion

Educators today are in an almost constant state of information overload (Hayakawa 1999). The average worker in the United States handles more than 200 messages a day in the form of phone calls, emails, faxes, postal mail, and interoffice mail (Bentley 2000). Technology is changing "what we listen to, whom we listen to, and how we listen" (Bentley 2000, 129). In the past when we listened, we were generally face-to-face with the speaker, or at least were listening live. Now, however, much of our communication—email, voice mail, and the like—is not in person or doesn't occur in real time (Wolvin & Coakley 2000).

Even when we are listening in real time, on a cell phone, for example, listening has become more multi-layered. During a cell phone conversation, we expect the speaker to be doing something else. If we find out what that is, it creates a certain impression; we might think differently about someone who is talking to us while at the beach, versus mowing the lawn, versus attending an international conference. Whether we think about it consciously or not, during the conversation we assess what the speaker is saying as well as what she is *not* saying because of where she is or whom she is with. So technology has changed not only the tools we use to listen, but also when and where we use them, and even what we think about as we listen.

Learning to Listen, Listening to Learn

In our overloaded, fast-paced world, modern views of listening competence focus on two dimensions:

> *Appropriateness* requires that listeners understand the content of the interaction and avoid violating conversation norms or rules excessively. *Effectiveness* requires that interaction goals be met or needs, desires, and intentions are satisfied. Listening competency, then, requires successfully adapting to situations and achieving intended or desired results through communication. (Bentley 2000, 138, italics added)

Thus, it is no longer sufficient to "get the message"; rather, the expectation is that taking the time to listen will shape our relationships (Cooper 1997). By listening attentively to children, their families, and our colleagues, early childhood educators are forging the kinds of connections that produce high-quality programs for the very young.

References

Addressing audio needs of every learner. 2004. *Media & Methods* 41 (3): 40.

Adelmann, K. 2005. Listening and referring to voices: Students' repertory in educational settings. *International Journal of Listening* 15: 38–67.

American Academy of Pediatrics, Committee on Public Education. 2007. *Children, adolescents, and television*. Online: http://aappolicy.aappublications.org/cgi/reprint/pediatrics;107/2/423.pdf.

American Society for Deaf Children. 2007. ASDC Snap Shots: "I suspect my baby has a hearing loss—what should I do?" Online: http://deafchildren.org/resources/7_I%20Suspect%20my%20Baby%20has%20a%20Hearing%20Loss.pdf.

American Speech-Language-Hearing Association. 2004. *Hearing, Noise, and School-Aged Children*. Brochure. Rockville, MD: Author.

American Speech-Language-Hearing Association. 2007a. *Assistive Technology*. Rockville, MD: ASHA. Online: http://www.asha.org/public/hearing/treatment/assist_tech.htm.

American Speech-Language-Hearing Association. 2007b. *How does your child hear and talk?* Slide wheel/developmental chart. Rockville, MD: Author.

Anderson, R.C., E.H. Hiebert, J.A. Scott, & I.A.G. Wilkinson. 1985. *Becoming a nation of readers: The report of the Commission on Reading*. Washington, DC: United States Office of Education.

Annett, M.M. 2004. Building foundations for literacy. *ASHA Leader* 9 (1): 12.

Anthony, J.L., & C.J. Lonigan. 2004. The nature of phonological awareness: Converging evidence from four studies of preschool and early grade school children. *Journal of Educational Psychology* 96 (1): 1–18.

Apel, K., & J. Masterson. 2001. *Beyond baby talk*. Sparks, NY: Prima Publishing.

Armbruster, B.B., F. Lehr, & J. Osborn. 2003. *A child becomes a reader: Kindergarten through grade 3*. 2d ed. Washington, DC: National Institute for Literacy.

Aukerman, A. 2006. Who's afraid of the big "bad answer"? *Educational Leadership* 64 (2): 37–41.

Baker, A.C., & L.A. Manfredi/Petitt. 2004. *Relationships, the heart of quality care: Creating community among adults in early care settings*. Washington, DC: NAEYC.

Barker, L.L., & K.W. Watson. 2000. *Listen up*. New York: St. Martin's Press.

Barone, D.M., & L.M. Morrow. 2002. *Literacy and young children: Research-based practices*. New York: Guilford.

Bayless, K.M., & M.E. Ramsey. 1990. *Music: A way of life for the young child*. New York: Macmillan.

Bell, B. 2000. Listening. *Lessons in lifemanship*. Online: http://www.bbll.com/ch02.html.

Bennett-Armistead, V.S., N.K. Duke, & A.M. Moses. 2005. *Literacy and the youngest learner: Best practices for educators of children from birth to 5*. New York: Scholastic Teaching Resources.

Bentley, S.C. 2000. Listening in the 21st century. *International Journal of Listening* 14: 129–142.

Bergen, D. 2001. *Pretend play and young children's development*. ERIC Digest, ED458045. Online: www.ericdigests.org/2002-2/play.htm.

Bergman, O. 2005. *Wait for me!: Reader control of narration rate in talking books*. Online: http://www.readingonline.org/articles/art_index.asp?HREF=bergman/index.html.

Birbili, M. 2006. Mapping knowledge: Concept maps in early childhood education. *Early Childhood Research & Practice* 8 (2). Online: http://ecrp.uiuc.edu/v8n2/birbili.html.

Bishop, K., & M.A. Kimball. 2006. Engaging students in storytelling. *Teacher Librarian* 33 (4): 28–31.

Black, S. 2001. Thinking about teaching. *American School Board Journal* 108 (1): 42–44.

Bloome, D., et al. 2001. Spoken and written narrative development: African American preschoolers as storytellers and storymakers. In *Literacy in African American communities*, eds. J.L. Harris, et al., 45–76. Mahwah, NJ: Lawrence Erlbaum Associates.

Bommelje, R., J.M. Houston, & R. Smither. 2003. Personality characteristics of effective listeners: A five-factor perspective. *International Journal of Listening* 17: 32–46.

Braunger, J., & J.P. Lewis. 2005. *Building a knowledge base in reading*. 2d ed. Portland, OR: Northwest Regional Laboratory.

Bredekamp, S. 2000. *What early childhood teachers need to know about language*. ERIC, EDOFL0007. Online: http://www.cal.org/resources/digest/0007bredekamp.html.

Brent, R., & P. Anderson. 1993. Developing children's classroom listening strategies. *Reading Teacher* 47 (2): 122–126.

Brigman, G., D. Lane, & D. Switzer. 2001. Teaching children school success skills. *The Journal of Educational Research* 92 (6): 323–329.

Brown, P.M., F.W. Rickards, & A. Bortoli. 2001. Structures underpinning pretend play and word production in young hearing children and children with hearing loss. *Journal of Deaf Studies & Deaf Education* 6 (1): 15–31.

Brown, S.L. 1991. *Improving listening skills in young children*. ERIC, ED339058.

Bryan, T., & K. Burstein. 2004. Improving homework completion and academic performance: Lessons from special education. *Theory Into Practice* 43 (3): 213–219.

Buckleitner, W. 2000. Listen up. *Early Childhood Today* 15 (2): 9.

Burley-Allen, M. 1995. *Listening: The forgotten skill: A self-teaching guide*. Hoboken, NJ: John Wiley & Sons.

Burns, D.D. 1999. *The feeling good handbook*. New York: Plume.

Bushman, J., & W. Buster. 2002. Listen and learn. *Leadership* 31 (3): 30–33, 38.

Cain, K., & J. Oakhill. 2006. Profiles of children with specific reading comprehension difficulties. *British Journal of Educational Psychology* 76: 683–696.

Cassell, J. 2004. Towards a model of technology and literacy development: Story listening systems. *Journal of Applied Developmental Psychology* 25 (1): 75–105.

Church, E.B. 2006. Creating community at group time. *Early Childhood Today* 21 (1): 44–47.

Comer, L.B., & T. Drollinger. 1999. Active empathetic listening and selling success: A conceptual framework. *The Journal of Personal Selling and Sales Management* 19: 5–29.

Conderman, G., & J. Morin. 2004. Reflect upon your practice. *Intervention in School and Clinic* 40 (2): 111–115.

Cook-Cottone, C. 2004. Constructivism in family literacy practices: Parents as mentors. *Reading Improvement* 41 (4): 208–216.

Cooper, L.O. 1997. Listening competency in the workplace: A model for training. *Business Communication Quarterly* 60 (4): 75–85.

Copland, A. 1996. *Music and imagination.* Cambridge, MA: Harvard University Press. Quoted in: D. Wheeler. 1999. Lessons in listening. *Clavier* 38 (6): 8.

Couchenour, D., & K. Chrisman. 2003. *Families, schools and communities: Together for young children.* Clifton Park, NY: Thomson Delmar Learning.

Courage, M.K., & M.L. Howe. 2004. Advances in early memory development research: Insights about the dark side of the moon. *Developmental Review* 24: 6–32.

Crain-Thorenson, C. 1996. Phonemic processes in children's listening and reading comprehension. *Applied Cognitive Psychology* 10: 383–401.

Cramond, B. 1998. Speaking and listening: Key components of a complete language arts program. *Roeper Review* 16 (1): 44–49.

Crandell, C. 1996. Effects of sound-field FM amplification on the speech perception of ESL children. *Educational Audiology Monograph* 4 (1): 1–5.

Crncec, R., S. Wilson, & M. Prior. 2006. The cognitive and academic benefits of music to children: Facts and fictions. *Educational Psychology* 26 (4): 579–594.

Cruger, M. 2005. Language abilities and the impact of language difficulties. *The Parent Letter* 3 (7): 1–2. Online: http://www.aboutourkids.org/aboutour/parent_letter/2005/english_parent_letter_mar_05.pdf.

Cummins, J. 2003. *Bilingual Children's Mother Tongue: Why Is It Important for Education?* University of Toronto. Online: http://www.iteachilearn.com/cummins/mother.htm.

Darling, S., & L. Westberg. 2004. Parent involvement in children acquisition of reading. *The Reading Teacher* 58: 774–776.

Darling-Hammond, L., & O. Ifill-Lynch. 2006. If they'd only do their work! *Educational Leadership* 63 (5): 8–13.

David, J., O. Onchonga, R. Drew, R. Grass, R. Stuchuk, & M.S. Burns. 2006. Head Start embraces language diversity. *Young Children* 60 (6): 40–43.

De l'Etoile, S.K. 2006. Infant behavioral responses to infant-directed singing and other maternal interactions. *Infant behavior and development* 29 (3): 456–470.

DeAnda, I. 2000. Glasses for the ears: Technology provides a critical link to literacy. *Multimedia Schools* 7 (2): 48–52.

DeCasper, A.J., J.P. Lecanuet, M.C. Busnel, C. Granier-Deferre, & R. Maugeais. 1994. Fetal reactions to recurrent maternal speech. *Infant Behavior and Development* 17: 159–164.

DeVilliers, J. 1990. *Language processing and language acquisition.* New York: Springer Verlag.

Diamond, M., & J. Hopson. 1998. *Magic trees of the mind: How to nurture your child's intelligence, creativity, and healthy emotions from birth through adolescence.* New York: Penguin/Putnam.

Dockrell, J., M. Stuart, & D. King. 2004. Supporting early oral language skills. *Literacy Today* (September): 16–17.

Dougherty, D.P. 1999. *How to talk to your baby.* New York: Avery.

Dougherty, D.P., & D. Paul. 2007. *Talking on the go.* Rockville, MD: ASHA.

Dyson, A.H. 1987. The value of "time off task": Young children's spontaneous talk and deliberate text. *Harvard Educational Review* 57: 396–420.

Easterbrooks, S.R., & E.L. Estes. 2007. *Helping deaf and hard of hearing students to use spoken language: A guide for educators and families.* Thousand Oaks, CA: Corwin Press.

Eisenberg, L.S., N.E. Fink, & J.K. Niparko. 2006. Childhood development after cochlear implantation. *ASHA Leader* 11 (16): 5, 28–29.

Ertmer, D.J., & J.A. Mellon. 2001. Beginning to talk at 20 months: Early vocal development in a young cochlear implant recipient. *Journal of Speech, Language, and Hearing Research* 44 (1): 192–206.

Fernald, A., D. Swingley, & J.P. Pinto. 2001. When half a word is enough: Infants can recognize spoken words using partial phonetic information. *Child Development* 72 (4): 1003–1015.

Ferraro, J. 2000. *Reflective practice and professional development.* Washington, DC: ERIC Clearinghouse on Teaching and Teacher Education. ERIC, ED449120.

Fields, M.V., L. Groth, & K. Spangler. 2007. *Let's begin reading right.* 6th ed. Upper Saddle River, NJ: Prentice Hall.

Finn, J.D. 1998. Parental engagement that makes a difference. *Educational Leadership* 55 (8): 20–24.

Flexer, C. 1997. Individual sound-field systems: Rationale, description, and use. *The Volta Review* 99 (3): 133–157.

Floor, P., & N. Akhtar. 2006. Can 18-month-old infants learn words by listening to conversations? *Infancy* 9 (3): 327–339.

Floyd, J. 1985. *Listening: A practical approach.* Glenview, IL: Scott, Foresman.

Fraser, J., & D. Skolnick. 1994. *On their way: Celebrating second graders as they read and write.* Portsmouth, NH: Heinemann.

Funk, H., & G.D. Funk. 1989. Guidelines for developing listening skills. *The Reading Teacher* 42: 660–664.

Gallas, K. 1994. *The languages of learning: How children talk, write, dance, and sing their understanding of the world.* New York: Teachers College Press.

Gallenstein, N. 2005. Never too young for a concept map. *Science and Children* 43 (1): 44–47.

Garman, C.G., & J.F. Garman. 1992. *Teaching young children effective listening skills.* York, PA: William Gladden Foundation.

Garmston, R.J. 2005. *The presenter's fieldbook: A practical guide.* Norwood, MA: Christopher-Gordon.

Gartrell, D. 2006. Guidance Matters: Build relationships through talk. *Young Children* 61 (5): 50–52.

Gazdag, G., & S.F. Warren. 2000. Effects of adult contingent imitation on development of young children's vocal imitation. *Journal of Early Intervention* 23 (1): 24–35.

Gilbert, M.B. 2005. An examination of listening effectiveness of educators: Performance and preference. *Professional Educator* 27 (1): 1–18.

Goh, C., & Y. Taib. 2006. Metacognitive instruction in listening for young learners. *ELT Journal: English Language Teachers Journal* 60 (3): 222–232.

Gonzalez-Mena, J. 1998. *The child in the family and the community*. 2d ed. Upper Saddle River, NJ: Merrill/Prentice Hall.

Goodwin, S.W., & L.P. Accredolo. 2000. *Baby minds*. New York: Bantam.

Gregg, G. 1983. "They have ears, but hear not": Would a course in listening help? *Across the Board* (September): 56–61.

Griffiths, P. 1986. Early vocabulary. In *Language Acquisition: Studies in first language development*, 2d ed., eds. P. Fletcher & M. Garman. New York: Cambridge University Press.

Groce, R.D. 2004. An experimental study of elementary teachers with the storytelling process: Interdisciplinary benefits associated with teacher training and classroom integration. *Reading Improvement* 41 (2): 122–128.

Grover, S., & L. Hannegan. 2005. Not Just for Listening. *Book Links* 14: 16–20.

Gunning, T.G. 1995. Word Building: A strategic approach to the teaching of phonics. *Reading Teacher* 48 (6): 484–488.

Haden, C.A., P.A. Ornstein, & S.M. Didow. 2001. Mother-child conversational interchanges as events unfold: Linkages to subsequent remembering. *Child Development* 72: 1016–1031.

Hale-Benson, J.E. 1986. *Black children: Their roots, culture, and learning style*. Baltimore: Johns Hopkins University Press.

Hayakawa, S.I. 1999. The task of the listener: (Retrospect) analysis of skepticism. *ETC.: A Review of General Semantics* 56: 110–112.

Hearing, Speech, and Deafness Center. 2007. *Ear infections and speech development*. Online: http://www.hsdc.org/News/Speech/earinfections.htm.

Heath, S.M., & J.H. Hogben. 2004. Cost-effective prediction of reading difficulties. *Journal of Speech, Language, and Hearing Research* 47: 751–765.

Heller, M.F. 2007. Telling stories and talking facts: First graders' engagements in a nonfiction book club. *Reading Teacher* 60 (4): 358–369.

Hendrick, J., & P. Weissman. 2005. *The whole child: Developmental education for the early years*. 8th ed. Upper Saddle River, NJ: Prentice Hall.

Hill-Clarke, K.Y., & N.R. Robinson. 2004. It's as easy as A-B-C and do-re-mi: Music, rhythm, and rhyme enhance children's literacy skills. *Young Children* 59 (5): 91–95.

Holum, A., & J. Gahala. 2001. *Critical Issue: Using technology to enhance literacy instruction*. North Central Regional Educational Laboratory. Online: http://www.ncrel.org/sdrs/areas/issues/content/cntareas/reading/li300.htm.

Hoot, J.L., T. Szecsi, & S. Moosa. 2003. What teachers of young children should know about Islam. *Early Childhood Education Journal* 31 (2): 85–90.

Horn, M. 2005. Listening to Nysia: Storytelling as a way into writing in kindergarten. *Language Arts* 83 (1): 33–41.

Hunsaker, R.A. 1990. *Understanding and developing the skills of oral communication: Speaking and listening*. 2d ed. Englewood, CO: Morton.

Hyslop, N.B., & B. Tone. 1988. *Listening: Are we teaching it, and if so, how?* ERIC, ED295132.

Hyson, M., K. Hirsh-Pasek, & L. Rescorla. 1990. The classroom practices inventory: An observation instrument based on NAEYC's guidelines for developmentally appropriate practices for 4- and 5-year-old children. *Early Childhood Research Quarterly* 5: 475–493.

Imhof, M. 2002. In the eye of the beholder: Children's perception of good and poor listening behavior. *International Journal of Listening* 16: 40–56.

Imhof, M. 2004. Who are we as we listen? Individual listening profiles in varying contexts. *International Journal of Listening* 16: 36–45.

International Listening Association. 1995. An ILA definition of listening. *Listening Post* 53: 4.

International Listening Association. 2005. *Listening Facts*. Online: http://www.listen.org/Templates/facts.htm.

Isbell, R., J. Sobel, L. Lindauer, A. Lowrance. 2004. The effects of storytelling and story reading on the oral language complexity and story comprehension of young children. *Early Childhood Education Journal* 32 (3): 157–163.

Isenberg, J.P., & M.R. Jalongo. 2007. *Creative thinking and arts-based learning, K–4*. Upper Saddle River, NJ: Prentice Hall.

Jalongo, M.R. 1991. *Strategies for developing children's listening skills*. Bloomington, IN: Phi Delta Kappa.

Jalongo, M.R. 1995. Promoting active listening in the classroom. *Childhood Education* 72 (1): 13–18.

Jalongo, M.R., ed. 2003. *The world's children and their companion animals: Developmental and educational significance of the child/pet bond*. Olney, MD: Association for Childhood Education International.

Jalongo, M.R. 2006. *Early childhood language arts*. 4th ed. Boston: Allyn & Bacon.

Janusik, L. 2002. Teaching listening: What do we do? What should we do? *International Journal of Listening* 16 (5): 5–39.

Jensen, E. 1998. *Teaching with the brain in mind*. Alexandria, VA: Association for Supervision and Curriculum Development.

Jensen, E. 2006. *Enriching the brain: How to maximize every learner's potential*. San Francisco, CA: Jossey-Bass.

Jerger, J. 2006. Auditory processing disorders in children. *Journal of the American Academy of Audiology* 17 (5): 1–2.

Johnson, J., & M. Koga. 2006/2007. The art of listening with depth, understanding, flow, and imagery. *American Music Teacher* 56 (3): 22–27.

Jusczyk, P.W. 2000. *The discovery of spoken language*. Cambridge, MA: MIT Press.

Justice, L.M., J. Meier, & S. Walpole. 2005. Learning new words from storybooks: An efficacy study with at-risk kindergartners. *Language, Speech, & Hearing Services in Schools* 36 (1): 17.

Kamp, L.K. 2006. Listening to understand. *Liberal Education* 92 (2): 34–45.

Kendall, F. 1996. *Diversity in the classroom: New approaches to the education of young children*. New York: Teachers College Press.

Kenedeou, P., J. Lynch, P. van den Broek, C.A. Espin, M.J. White, & K.E. Kremer. 2005. Developing successful readers: Building early comprehension skills through television viewing and listening. *Early Childhood Education Journal* 33 (2): 91–98.

Kerry, T. 1982. *Effective questioning*. London: Macmillan.

Kiewitz, C., J.B. Weaver, III, H.B. Brosius, & G. Weinmann. 1997. Cultural differences in listening styles preferences: A comparison of young adults in Germany, Israel, and the United States. *International Journal of Public Opinion Research* 9 (3): 233–247.

Kirkland, L.D., & J. Patterson. 2005. Developing oral language in primary classrooms. *Early Childhood Education Journal* 32 (6): 391–395.

Kirkpatrick, D.L. 2007. Listening Quotation Archives. International Listening Association. Online: http://www.listen.org/quotations/morequotes.html.

Konecki, L.R. 1992. *"Parent Talk": Helping families to relate to schools and facilitate children's learning*. Bloomington, IN: Phi Delta Kappa. ERIC, ED342745.

Krashen, S.D. 1988. *Second language acquisition and learning*. Englewood Cliffs, NJ: Prentice Hall.

Krashen, S.D. 2003. *Explorations in language acquisition and use*. Portsmouth, NH: Heinemann.

Kratcoski, A.M., & K.B. Katz. 1998. Conversing with young language learners in the classroom. *Young Children* 53 (3): 30–33.

Lapadat, J.C. 2002. Relationships between instructional language and primary students' learning. *Journal of Educational Psychology* 94 (2): 278–290.

Lonigan, C.J. 2005. *Development and promotion of early literacy skills: Using data to help children succeed*. Online: http://www.ncld.org/index.php?option=content&task=view&id=506.

Lu, M.Y. 2000. *Language development in the early years*. ERIC, ED446336. Online: http://www.vtaide.com/png/ERIC/Language-Early.htm.

Lucia, A. 1997. Leaders know how to listen. *HR Focus* 74 (4): 25.

Marschark, M. 2007. *Psychological development of deaf children*. New York: Oxford University Press.

Mason, J.M., & K.H. Au. 1998. *Reading instruction for today*. Reading, MA: Addison-Wesley.

McCormick, L., D.F. Loeb, & R.L. Schiefelbusch. 2002. *Supporting children with communication difficulties in inclusive settings: School-based language intervention*. 2d ed. Boston: Allyn & Bacon.

McDevitt, T.M. 1990. Encouraging young children's listening. *Academic Therapy* 25 (5): 569–577.

McDevitt, T.M., & J.E. Ormrod. 2007. *Child development and education*. 3d ed. Upper Saddle River, NJ: Prentice Hall.

McInnes, A., T. Humphries, S. Hogg-Johnson, & R. Tannock. 2003. Listening comprehension and working memory are impaired in attention-deficit hyperactivity disorder irrespective of language impairment. *Journal of Abnormal Child Psychology* 31 (4): 428–445.

McNeill, J.H., & S.A. Fowler. 1996. Using story reading to encourage children's conversations. *Teaching Exceptional Children* 28 (4): 43–47.

McSporran, E. 1997. Towards better listening and learning in the classroom. *Educational Review* 49 (1): 13–21.

Mediatore, K. 2003. Reading with your ears. *Reference & User Services Quarterly* 42 (4): 318–323.

Mehler, J., & E. Dupoux. 1994. *What infants know*. Cambridge, MA: Blackwell.

Mercer, N. 1995. *The guided construction of knowledge: Talk amongst teachers and learners*. Clevedon, UK: Multilingual Matters Ltd.

Merkel-Piccini, R. 2001. Listening to learn. *ASHA Super-Duper Handy Handouts!* 10. Online: http://www.superduperinc.com/handouts/pdfs/6/listeningto learn.pdf.

Messiou, K. 2006. Conversations with children: Making sense of marginalization. *European Journal of Special Needs Education* 21 (1): 39–54.

Miller, D.C. 2007. *Essentials of school neuropsychological assessment*. Hoboken, NJ: John Wiley & Sons.

Milne, A.A. 2004. *Now we are six* (New edition). London: Egmont Books Ltd.

Minskoff, E. 2005. *Teaching reading to struggling learners*. Baltimore: Paul H. Brookes.

Murray, T., & J. Swartz. 1989. Now hear this: Six activities designed to sharpen the listening skills of auditory learners. *Teaching PreK–8* 19: 58–60.

Music Educators National Conference. 1994. *Opportunity-to-learn standards for music instruction: Grades PreK–12.* Online: http://www.menc.org/publication/books/otl.html.

NAEYC. 1994. Tribute to Loris Malaguzzi. *Young Children* 49 (5): 55.

NAEYC. 1997. Developmentally appropriate practice in early childhood programs serving children from birth though age 8. Position Statement, adopted July 1996. In *Developmentally appropriate practice in early childhood programs*, rev. ed., eds. S. Bredekamp & C. Copple, 3–30. Washington, DC: Author.

Napoli, D.J. 2003. *Language matters: A guide to everyday questions about language.* New York: Oxford University Press.

Nation, I.S.P. 2006. How large a vocabulary is needed for reading and listening. *Canadian Modern Language Review* 63 (1): 59–82.

Nation, K., & M.J. Snowling. 2004. Beyond phonological skills: Broader language skills contribute to the development of reading. *Journal of Research in Reading* 27 (4): 342–356.

National Center for Education Statistics [NCES]. 2002. *Early childhood longitudinal study: Kindergarten class of 1998–99.* Washington, DC: U.S. Department of Education, Office of Educational Research and Improvement. Online: http://www.nces.ed.gov/ecls/Kindergarten.asp.

National Communication Association. 1998. *The speaking, listening, and media literacy standards and competency statements for K–12 education.* Online: http://www.natcom.org/nca/files/ccLibraryFiles/FILENAME/000000000119/K12%20Standards.pdf.

National Research Council, Committee on Early Childhood Pedagogy. 2001. *Eager to learn: Educating our preschoolers.* Washington, DC: National Academy Press.

Naudé, H., E. Pretorius, & J. Viljoen. 2003. The impact of impoverished language development on preschoolers' readiness-to-learn during the Foundation Phase. *Early Child Development & Care* 173: 271–292.

Nelson, K. 2007. *Young minds in social worlds: Experience, meaning and memory.* Cambridge, MA: Harvard University Press.

Nelson, K.E., A. Aksu-Koc, & C.E. Johnson, eds. 2001. *Children's language: Developing narrative and discourse competence.* Mahwah, NJ: Lawrence Erlbaum Associates.

Nespeca, S.M. 2005. Join in! Picture books that invite participation. *Book Links* (May): 48–51.

Nichols, R.G., & L.A. Stevens. 1957a. *Are you listening?* New York: McGraw-Hill.

Nichols, R.G., & L.A. Stevens. 1957b. Listening to people. *Harvard Business Review* 35: 112–119.

Nichols, R.G., J.I. Brown, & R.J. Keller. 2006. Measurement of communication skills. *International Journal of Listening* 20: 13–17.

Nistler, R.J., & A. Maiers. 2000. Stopping the silence: Hearing parents' voices in an urban first-grade family literacy program. *The Reading Teacher* 53 (8): 670–680.

Norton, D.E. 2003. *The effective teaching of language arts.* 6th ed. Upper Saddle River, NJ: Prentice Hall.

Opitz, M.F., & M.D. Zbaracki. 2004. *Listen hear! 25 effective listening comprehension strategies.* Portsmouth, NH: Heinemann.

Paley, V.G. 2004. *Wally's stories* (Reprint edition). Cambridge, MA: Harvard University Press.

Palmer, S. 2004. Foundations of literacy. *Literacy Today* (March): 7.

Pantaleo, S. 2007. Interthinking: Young children using language to think collectively during interactive read-alouds. *Early Childhood Education Journal* 34 (6): 439–447.

Paquette, K.R., S. Fello, & M.R. Jalongo. 2007. The talking drawings strategy: Using primary children's illustrations and oral language to improve comprehension of expository text. *Early Childhood Education Journal* 35 (1): 65–73.

Paul, S. 1996. *The top 10 tips for becoming a better listener*. Online: http://topten.org/public/BN/BN12.html.

Pearson Education, Inc. 2007. *Peabody Picture Vocabulary Test*, 4th edition (PPVT-IV). Upper Saddle River, NJ: Pearson/American Guidance Services.

Petry, E., J. McClellan, & P. Myler. 2001. Listening and learning in classroom acoustical design. *The Journal of the Acoustical Society of America* 109 (5): 478.

Plourde, L. 1989. *Class preschool: Classroom listening and speaking—preschool*. Tucson, AZ: Communication Skill Builders.

Powers, W.G., & G.D. Bodie. 2003. Listening fidelity: Seeking congruence between cognitions of the listener and the sender. *International Journal of Listening* 17: 19–31.

Purdy, M. 2006. Ralph Nichols: A leader in and of his time. *International Journal of Listening* 20: 20–21.

Reid, L. 1991. Improving young children's listening by verbal self-regulation: The effect of mode of rule presentation. *The Journal of Genetic Psychology* 153 (4): 447–461.

Richgels, D.J. 2001. Invented spelling, phonemic awareness, and reading and writing instruction. In *Handbook of early literacy research*, eds. S.B. Neuman & D.K. Dickinson, 142–158. New York: Guilford.

Risko, V., K. Roskos, & C. Vukelich. 2002. Prospective teachers' reflection: Strategies, qualities, and perceptions in learning to teach reading. *Reading Research and Instruction* 41 (2): 149–175.

Rogers, C.L., J.J. Lister, D.M. Febo, J.M. Besing, & H.B. Abrams. 2006. Effects of bilingualism, noise, and reverberation on speech perception by listeners with normal hearing. *Applied Psycholinguistics* 27 (3): 465–485.

Rose, J., & the Rose Review Support Team. 2006. Phonics Final Report—The Rose Review. *Education Journal* 94: 28. Online: http://www.standards.dfes.gov.uk/rosereview.

Roskos, K., J.F. Christie, & D.J. Richgels. 2003. The essentials of early literacy instruction. *Young Children* 58 (2): 52–60.

Rule, A.C. 2007. Mystery boxes: Helping children improve their reasoning. *Early Childhood Education Journal* 35 (1): 13–18.

Rushton, S., & E. Larkin. 2001. Shaping the learning environment: Connecting developmentally appropriate practices to brain research. *Early Childhood Education Journal* 29 (1): 25–33.

Saffran, J.R., & G.J. Griepentrog. 2001. Absolute pitch in infant auditory learning: Evidence for developmental reorganization. *Developmental Psychology* 37 (1): 74–85.

Salyer, D.M. 1994. Noise or communication: Talking, writing, and togetherness in one first grade classroom. *Young Children* 49 (4): 42–47.

Saracho, O.N. 2002. Family literacy: Exploring family practices. *Early Child Development and Care* 172 (2): 113–122.

Saracho, O.N. 2007, in press. A literacy program for fathers: A case study. *Early Childhood Educational Journal* 35 (4).

Sargent, S.L., & J.B. Weaver, III. 2003. Listening styles: Sex differences in perceptions of self. *International Journal of Listening* 17: 5–18.

Schultz, K. 2003. *Listening: A framework for teaching across differences.* New York: Teachers College Press.

Seefeldt, C. 2005. *How to work with standards in early childhood classrooms.* New York: Teachers College Press.

Seo, K. 2002. Research note: The effect of visuals on listening comprehension: A study of Japanese learners' listening strategies. *International Journal of Listening* 16: 57–81.

Seplocha, H. 2007. Partnerships for learning: Conferencing with families. In *Spotlight on young children and families*, ed. D. Koralek, 12–15. Washington, DC: NAEYC.

Shidler-Lattz, L. 2002. Things that should make us go hmmm! Listening to what we say to children. *Young Children* 57: 92–94.

Shiver, E. 2002. *Brain development and mastery of language in the young years.* Online: http://www.parentinginformation.org/braindevelopment.htm.

Sims, W.L. 2005. Effects of free versus directed listening on duration of individual music listening by prekindergarten children. *Journal of Research in Music Education* 53 (1): 78–86.

Skouge, J.R., K. Rao, & C. Boisvert. 2007. Promoting early literacy for diverse learners using audio and video technology. *Early Childhood Education Journal* 35 (1): 5–11.

Slavin, R.E. 2005. *Educational psychology: Theory and practice.* 5th ed. Boston: Allyn & Bacon.

Smith, C.B. 2003. *Skills students use when speaking and listening.* Bloomington, IN: ERIC Clearinghouse on Reading, English, and Language. ERIC, ED480895.

Smith, F. 2003. *Unspeakable acts, unnatural practices: Flaws and fallacies in "scientific" reading instruction.* Portsmouth, NH: Heinemann.

Smith, P.G., ed. 2001. *Talking classrooms: Shaping children's learning through oral language instruction.* Newark, DE: IRA.

Steil, L.K., & R.K. Bommelje. 2004. *Listening leaders.* Edina, MN: Beaver's Pond Press.

Stevens, L., K. Watson, & K. Dodd. 2001. Supporting parents of children with communication difficulties: A model. *International Journal of Language and Communication Disorders* 55: 70–74.

Stone, C.A., E.R. Silliman, B.J. Ehren, & K. Apel, eds. 2005. *Handbook of language and literacy: Development and disorders.* New York: Guilford.

Swain, K., J.M. Harrington, & M. Friehe. 2004. Teaching listening strategies in the inclusive classroom. *Intervention in School & Clinic* 40: 48–55.

Szente, J. 2007. Empowering young children for success in school and life. *Early Childhood Education Journal* 34 (6): 449–453.

Tabors, P.O., & C.E. Snow. 2001. Young bilingual children and early literacy development. In *Handbook of early literacy research*, eds. S.B. Neuman & D.K. Dickinson, 159–178. New York: Guilford.

Thal, D.J., & M. Flores. 2001. Development of sentence interpretation strategies by typically developing and late-talking toddlers. *Journal of Child Language* 28 (1): 173–193.

Thomas, W.P., & V.T. Collier. 1997. *School effectiveness for language minority students.* Washington, DC: National Clearinghouse for Bilingual Education.

Timm, S., & B.L. Schroeder. 2000. Listening/nonverbal communication training. *International Journal of Listening* 12: 109–128.

Tomasello, M. 2003. *Constructing a language: A usage-based theory of language acquisition.* Cambridge, MA: Harvard University Press.

Tompkins, G.E. 2005. *Literacy for the 21st century: A balanced approach.* Upper Saddle River, NJ: Prentice Hall.

Torbert, M. 2005. Using active group games to develop basic life skills. *Young Children* 60 (4): 72–78.

Truesdale, S. 1990. Whole body listening: Developing active auditory skills. *Language, Speech and Hearing Services in School* 21: 183–184.

U.S. Census Bureau. 2007. *Statistical Abstract of the United States 2007.* Online: http://www.census.gov/compendia/statab/2007edition.html.

U.S. Department of Education. 2002. *Teaching our youngest: A guide for preschool teachers and child care and family providers.* Online: http://www.ed.gov/teachers/how/early/teachingouryoungest/index.html.

Uhry, J.K. 2002. Finger-point reading in kindergarten: The role of phonemic awareness, one-to-one correspondence, and rapid serial naming. *Scientific Studies of Reading* 6 (4): 319–342.

Vining, J.W., & A. Yrle. 1980. How do you rate as a listener? *Supervisory Management* 25: 22–25.

Vouloumanos, A., & J.F. Werker. 2007. Listening to language at birth: Evidence for a bias for speech in neonates. *Developmental Science* 10 (2): 159–164.

Wambacq, I.J.A., K. Shea-Miller, A.M. Eckert, & V. Toth. 2005. Perception of auditory movement in children with poor listening skills: An ERP Study. *Journal of the American Academy of Audiology* 16 (5): 312–326.

Ward, S. 2001. *Baby talk: Strengthen your child's ability to listen, understand, and communicate.* New York: Ballantine.

Warner, S.A. 1963. *Teacher.* New York: Touchstone Books.

Watson, K.W., L.L. Barker, & J.B. Weaver, III. 1995. The listening styles profile (LSP-16): Development and validation of an instrument to assess four listening styles. *International Journal of Listening* 9: 1–13.

Westene, H. 1997. Listening comprehension. *Journal of Educational Research* 68 (1): 30–33.

White, M. 2002. Teachers on teaching: A lesson on listening. *Young Children* 57 (3): 43.

Williams, G. 1992. Dance, language development, and the young child. *Early Child Development and Care* 79: 107–123.

Wolvin, A.D. 2006. Modeling listening scholarship. *International Journal of Listening* 20: 22–26.

Wolvin, A.D., & C.G. Coakley. 1996. *Listening.* 5th ed. New York: McGraw-Hill.

Wolvin, A.D., & C.G. Coakley. 2000. Listening education in the 21st century. *International Journal of Listening* 12: 143–152.

Wyatt, N. 1989. Structuring speaking and listening in the classroom. In *Talking to learn: Classroom practices in teaching English,* eds. D. Gallo, et al. Urbana, IL: National Council of Teachers of English.

Yaden, D.B., & J.R. Paratore. 2003. Family literacy at the turn of the millennium: The costly future of maintaining the status quo. In *Handbook of research on teaching the English language arts,* 2d ed., eds. J. Flood, D. Lapp, J.R. Squire, & J.M. Jensen, 532–545. Mahwah, NJ: Lawrence Erlbaum Associates.

Children's Books (and Recordings)

Buckwheat Zydeco. *Choo choo boogaloo.*

Carle, E. *The very hungry caterpillar.*

Fleischman, P. *Joyful noise: Poems for two voices.*

Harrison, D.L. *Farmer's garden: Rhymes for two voices.*

Holbrook, S. *Wham! It's a poetry jam: Discovering performance poetry.*

Kubler, A. *Head, shoulders, knees and toes.*

Mitton, T. *Down by the cool of the pool.*

Testa, F. *Wolf's favor.*

Williams, G. *Baby animals.*

Bibliography of Picture Books That Invite Careful Listening

by Melissa Ann Renck and Mary Renck Jalongo

Infant/Toddler

Andrews-Goebel, N. *The pot that Juan built*.
   A cumulative tale modeled after *The House That Jack Built* situated in Mexico.

Appelt, K. *Toddler two-step*.
   A rhyming text celebrates toddlers' creative movement in response to music.

Boston, C. *Jazz baby*.
   Several toddlers are inspired to hum, play, and move to a jazzy beat.

Cooke, T. *So much*.
   Members of the extended African American family arrive, all with their unique ways of showing and saying how much they love the baby.

DK Publishing. *Wheels on the bus*.
   The early childhood song gets an update as a board book with pop-ups and a sound chip.

Ehrlich, H.M. *Gotcha, Louie!*
   Little Louie listens so that he can play a chasing game with his mom at the beach.

O'Connell, R. *The baby goes beep*.
   A baby makes various sounds as he explores the world around him.

Neubecker, R. *Wow! City!*
   A toddler takes in the sights as she tours a city on her father's shoulders.

Potter, B. *Listen! Peter Rabbit.*
  This board book of the classic character is updated with a computer chip of various sounds.

Thong, R. *Tummy girl.*
  A captivating rhyme chronicles a very young child's growth and development

Walter, V. *"Hi, pizza man!"*
  A visitor is coming to the house and a young child wonders, who can it be? It's pizza home delivery!

Ward, C. *Cookie's week.*
  An entire week of feline misadventures, courtesy of Cookie, a black and white cat.

Preschool/Primary

Banks, K. *Close your eyes.*
  Although a young tiger cub is reluctant to take his nap, in this mood book, his mother has a reassuring answer to each of his objections.

Bee, W. *And the train goes…*
  A parrot at the train station listens in on passengers' talk and the sounds that the train makes.

Bruss, D. *Book! Book! Book!*
  A group of farm animals marches off to the library for storytime, led by a hen and her "book, book, book" clucking.

Campoy, F.I., & A.F. Ada. *Tales our abuelitas told: A Hispanic folktale collection.*
  An assortment of folktales that invites attentive listening.

Conrad, P. *Blue willow.*
  A wealthy and doting father realizes the importance of careful listening when his daughter, Kung Shi Fair, decides to marry.

Cumberbatch, J. *Can you hear the sea?*
  On her grandfather's advice, Sarah listens to a shell in hopes of hearing the sea.

Guy, G.F. *Siesta.*
  In this Spanish/English text and simple story, a brother and sister use common household items to set up an outdoor naptime with teddy.

Hopkins, L. *Wonderful words: Poems about reading, writing, speaking, and listening.*
  A poetry collection with numerous selections about listening.

Martin, B., Jr., & J. Archambault. *Listen to the rain*.
A favorite picture book author team urges children to listen carefully to sounds all around them.

Martin, B., Jr., M. Sampson, & L. Ehlert. *Chicka chicka 1, 2, 3*.
In this sequel to the alphabet book *Chicka Chicka Boom Boom*, the authors create another lively poem/chant, this time about counting.

McKissack, P. *Porch lies: Tales of slicksters, tricksters, and other wily characters*.
Sassy characters from the African American tradition intrigue listeners with their clever ways.

Page, R., & S. Jenkins. *What do you do with a tail like this?*
In this beautifully illustrated book, children participate in a guessing game about various animals' body parts and how they are used.

Pearson, D. *Big city song*.
Children are prompted to think about the sounds that are distinctive to life in the city.

Pfeffer, W. *Sounds all around*.
A nonfiction book about hearing and listening.

Poydar, N. *Bunny business*.
Harry's careful listening makes all the difference in the class play about rabbits.

Rathmann, P. *Officer Buckle and Gloria*.
A police officer's presentations on safety to schoolchildren are boring until his dog gets into the act.

Ravishankar, A. *Tiger on a tree*.
The chant-like text of this story about a tiger's visit to an Indian village includes many rhyming words that children can identify.

Reidy, H. *All sorts of noises*.
Draws children's attention to the sounds all around them.

Rylant, C. *Night in the country*.
Lyrical language and lovely illustrations invite children to regard night sounds in a reassuring way.

Showers, P. *The listening walk*.
A picture book classic about paying attention to everyday sounds.

Sharratt, N. *Shark in the park*.
A humorous rhyme about a boy with a telescope and his wildly imaginative interpretations of what he sees.

Shaw, N. *Sheep in a jeep*.
The humor and rhyme of this book created a series of misadventures from a crew of silly sheep.

Williams, B. *Albert's impossible toothache.*
   The only one who will really listen to Albert's complaint about his tooth is his grandmother.

Williams, S. *I went walking.*
   A walking tour of the farm keeps children guessing which animal they'll see next.

Wilson, K. *Bear wants more!*
   A bear emerges from hibernation with a ravenous appetite, and children can chime in with the refrain, "but bear wants more!"

Wolff, F. *It is the wind.*
   A baby is lulled to sleep by the calming sounds of animals in the evening.

*Melissa Ann Renck is the children's services librarian
at Toledo Lucas County Library.*

If you like this book, check out these titles from NAEYC!

Young Children and Picture Books (2d ed.)
Mary Renck Jalongo

When you share picture books with young children, you build their lifelong literacy and enjoyment of reading. In beautiful full color, the new edition of this popular book will help you recognize quality in children's literature and illustration and see how to use picture books to best advantage. Lists of recommended books are included. Item #160

Spotlight on Young Children and Language
Derry Koralek, ed.

Research confirms that a rich language environment in the early years is key to children's success in many areas. This beautiful and engaging collection of articles describes powerful ways teachers can promote oral language. Also includes a list of top subject resources and carefully designed questions and activities for reflection. Item #283

Early years are learning years

Become a member of NAEYC,
and help make them count!

Just as you help young children learn and grow, the National Association for the Education of Young Children—your professional organization—supports you in the work you love. NAEYC is the world's largest early childhood education organization, with a national network of local, state, and regional Affiliates. We are more than 100,000 members working together to bring high-quality early learning opportunities to all children from birth through age eight.

Since 1926, NAEYC has provided educational services and resources for people working with children, including:

• *Young Children*, the award-winning journal (six issues a year) for early childhood educators

• **Books, posters, brochures, and videos** to support your work with young children and families

• **The NAEYC Annual Conference**, which brings tens of thousands of people together from across the country and around the world to share their expertise and ideas on the education of young children

• **Insurance plans** for members and programs

• **A voluntary accreditation system** to help programs reach national standards for high-quality early childhood education

• **Young Children International** to promote global communication and information exchanges

• **www.naeyc.org**—a dynamic Web site with up-to-date information on all of our services and resources

To join NAEYC

To find a complete list of membership benefits and options or to join NAEYC online, visit **www.naeyc.org/membership.** Or you can mail this form to us.
(Membership must be for an individual, not a center or school.)

Name_____

Address_____

City_____State_____ ZIP _____

E-mail_____

Phone (H)_____(W) _____

❏ New member   ❏ Renewal ID #_____

Affiliate name/number _____

To determine your dues, you must visit **www. naeyc.org/membership** or call 800-424-2460, ext. 2002.

Indicate your payment option

❏ VISA ❏ MasterCard ❏ AmEx ❏ Discover

Card #_____ Exp. date _____

Cardholder's name _____

Signature_____

Note: By joining NAEYC you also become a member of your state and local Affiliates.

Send this form and payment to

NAEYC,
PO Box 97156
Washington, DC 20090-7156